Japanese Banking, Securities
and Anti-Monopoly Law

Japanese Banking, Securities and Anti-Monopoly Law

Edited by:

Hiroshi Oda

Associate Professor of Law, Tokyo University

R Geoffrey Grice

Baker & McKenzie, Hong Kong

Butterworths
London, Boston, Dublin, Edinburgh, Kuala Lumpur,
Singapore,. Sydney, Toronto, Wellington
1988

United Kingdom	Butterworth & Co (Publishers) Ltd, 88 Kingsway, LONDON WC2B 6AB and 61A North Castle Street, EDINBURGH EH2 3LJ
Australia	Butterworths Pty Ltd, SYDNEY, MELBOURNE, BRISBANE, ADELAIDE, PERTH, CANBERRA and HOBART
Canada	Butterworths Canada Ltd, TORONTO and VANCOUVER
Ireland	Butterworth (Ireland) Ltd, DUBLIN
Malaysia	Malayan Law Journal Sdn Bhd, KUALA LUMPUR
New Zealand	Butterworths of New Zealand Ltd, WELLINGTON and AUCKLAND
Singapore	Butterworth & Co (Asia) Pte Ltd, SINGAPORE
USA	Butterworths Legal Publishers, ST PAUL, Minnesota, SEATTLE, Washington, BOSTON, Massachusetts, AUSTIN, Texas and D & S Publishers, CLEARWATER, Florida

A CIP Catalogue record for this book is available from the British Library.

ISBN United Kingdom 0 406 10685 1
      United States   0 88063 264 X

Typeset by Latimer Trend & Company Ltd
Printed by Biddles Ltd; Guildford and King's Lynn

Preface

This book consists of a selection of papers delivered at the first Japanese Law Conference held at the Faculty of Law, University College London in September 1987. That conference was the first event in a major programme on Japanese Law which was launched in April of the same year. The programme will consist of a Chair of Japanese Law and related developments at University College London and various exchange schemes. The programme has already been generously funded by more than fifty Japanese companies, and British institutions are, happily, now following suit.

We at UCL were delighted by the interest in this first conference. Although put on at short notice, it was attended by over fifty participants over five afternoons. Those attending underlined the urgent necessity for a programme that will contribute to the mutual understanding of our respective legal systems. UCL is determined to ensure the success of the programme by building on its links with the practising profession, industry and City of London institutions and its strong comparative orientation.

We are extremely grateful to Professor Hiroshi Oda, who organised the conference while on leave from the University of Tokyo as a Visiting Professor at University College London. Also to Geoffrey Grice for jointly editing these papers with Hiroshi Oda. Special thanks go to Baker & McKenzie for their support, to the Japan Information Centre of the Japanese Embassy, the Japan Export Trade Organisation (JETRO) and His Excellency Toshio Yamazaki, former Japanese Ambassador, who so warmly supported our programme.

22 August 1988

Professor Jeffrey Jowell
Head of Department
Faculty of Laws
University College London

List of contributors

Yūichi Ezawa; Director, Banking Inspection Department, Banking Bureau, Ministry of Finance.
Masabumi Yamane; General Manager and Head of the Legal Department, Bank of Tokyo. Author of *An Introduction to American Commercial Law* (Tokyo, 1987) (in Japanese).
Hiroshi Kinoshita; Partner, Tokyo Aoyama Law Office. JD (Columbia).
Takahira Ogawa; Economist, Nikko Research Center Ltd, London.
Osamu Kurihara; General Manager, IBJ International.
Shinichi Saito; Partner, Tokyo Aoyama Law Office.
Robert F Grondine; Partner, Tokyo Aoyama Law Office.
Masanao Nakagawa; Administrative Law Judge, Fair Trade Commission of Japan. Author of *Anti-Monopoly Legislation of Japan* (Tokyo, 1984).

Editors

Hiroshi Oda; Associate Professor, Faculty of Law, University of Tokyo. LLD (Tokyo).
R Geoffrey Grice; Solicitor, Baker & McKenzie, Hong Kong.

The views of the editors and contributors do not necessarily reflect those of the institution or firms to which they are affiliated.

Contents

I. Financial Law

Deregulation of the Japanese financial market and internationalization of the yen

Yūichi Ezawa
Director, Banking Inspection Department
Banking Bureau, Ministry of Finance

1. History and background

The 1980s has been a period of world-wide deregulation and integration of financial markets. Although the background differs from country to country, strong market forces are working in each market to push forward such development. In Japan, liberalization and internationalization of the Japanese financial market had been going on for several years. The Japanese Foreign Exchange and Foreign Trade Control Law was totally revised in 1980 and since then foreign exchange transactions are free to be made and subject to government control only in exceptional circumstances.[1] The Banking Law was also revised in 1981 so that banks could adapt to the new developments in the financial market.[2] Such developments, however, were greatly accelerated during the last four years, after two important documents were made public.

The so-called Japan-US Yen-Dollar Committee was set up at the time of President Reagan's visit to Japan in November 1983. The joint press announcement at that time by Treasury Secretary Regan and Finance Minister Takeshita pointed out that 'open and liberalized capital markets and free movement of capital are important to the operation of an effectively functioning international monetary system.' A working group was started consequently, chaired by Mr Oba, then the Japanese Vice-Minister of Finance, and Dr Sprinkel, then Under-Secretary of the US Treasury to discuss and work out a detailed plan. They submitted the so-called Yen-Dollar Report in May 1984.

At about the same time, the Japanese Ministry of Finance made public another document entitled 'The Current Status and Future Prospects for the Liberalization of Financial Markets and Internationalization of the Yen', which is less known but as significant as the Yen-Dollar Report. The Japanese

---

[1] A. D. Smith, 'The Japanese Foreign Exchange and Foreign Trade Control Law and Administrative Guidance: the Labyrinth and the Castle', *Law and Policy in International Business* (vol 16, 1984) pp 440–456.
[2] B. W. Semkow, 'Japanese Banking Law: Current Deregulation and Liberalization of Domestic and External Financial Transaction', *Law and Policy in International Business* (1985, No 1) p 81ff.

government had been making studies for some time on what its future course should be for liberalization and internationalization of the Japanese financial markets under the changing domestic and international environment. It was intended to provide the public with a better understanding of where Japan is heading.

Since then, policy statements have been made by the Japanese government in July 1985 and June 1987, in order to give future prospects of the financial market based on the measures already taken.

All these developments indicate that economic pressures were building up for liberalization and internationalization of the financial market. In the present author's view, they were the main driving force behind these developments, and the US and other foreign requests only helped accelerate the process.

The economic background which induced liberalization and internationalization of the Japanese financial market can be summarized in the following way.[3]

First, the Japanese economy, after experiencing two-digit growth rates in the 1960s and early 1970s, has shifted to a more stable growth pattern of 3–5%. During the period of the post-war economic development and the following rapid growth, financial resources were scarce and credit rationing under controlled interest rates was unavoidable. But now, as the economy slowed down, Japanese companies have large undistributed profits as surplus reserves. Liquidity is ample. They make every effort to reduce funding costs and increase returns on portfolios by diversifying methods and instruments of financing. Thus, people become very sensitive to interest rate changes and demand better services from financial institutions.

Secondly, in order to tide over the recessions caused by the two oil crises and also to play somewhat a more active role in the world economy, the Japanese government resorted to a large scale deficit spending since 1975. Outstanding government bonds, therefore, now amount to 51% of the GNP or 1 trillion dollars equivalent. Consequently, a huge secondary market has developed for the government bonds. The trading volume for the government bonds in cash alone amounted to 14 trillion dollars equivalent in 1986. With the development of such a large and free government bonds market, other financial markets cannot remain isolated and tightly regulated.

Thirdly, capital transactions in and out of Japan have increased enormously. Net outflow of long-term capital from Japan amounted to 130 billion dollars in 1986. They represent portfolio investments in foreign bonds and stocks, bank loans to foreign governments and corporations and overseas direct investments. As international capital transactions increase, they bring about competition between foreign and domestic financial markets and cannot but push the domestic markets toward further liberalization.

[3] As for the economic background, see the articles in Y. Suzuki, ed, *The Japanese Financial System* (Oxford, 1987).

2. Deregulation of the domestic financial market

When discussing the deregulation of Japanese financial markets, there are three important areas that require attention; deregulation of the domestic market, improvement of foreign access to the domestic market and growth of the Euro-yen market. The domestic market is built on a long history and any change of its basic framework is not easy. Substantial progress, however, is taking place in such areas as deregulation of interest rates and development of short-term money markets, while a review of the existing institutional framework is now being undertaken.[4]

DEREGULATION OF INTEREST RATE CEILING

In Japan, interest rates on deposits have been regulated by the Bank of Japan guidelines, which determines the maximum rate of interest banks can pay. However, such instruments as negotiable certificates of deposits (CD's), money market certificates (MMC's), or foreign-currency denominated deposits, which are free from interest rate ceilings, have been introduced in recent years. Furthermore, very important steps are being taken to deregulate the interest rates on large-denomination time deposits in general.

Japan is deregulating the interest rates on deposits from large-denomination and short-term deposits. CD's, free from interest rate ceilings, were introduced in 1979 with a minimum denomination of 500 million yen (approx 4 million dollars). This has been reduced gradually from 500 million yen to 300 million yen and to 100 million yen. Their maturity range has been widened from three to six months to one to six months and further extended to one year. MMC's were introduced in March 1985, which were deposits of 50 million yen or more, the interest rate of which is determined based on the CD market interest rate. The minimum size was reduced to 30 million yen and then to 20 million, and will be 10 million yen (approx 80 thousand dollars) by October 1987. The maximum maturity was extended from six months to two years.

The most important step in this respect is the deregulation of interest rates on large denomination deposits which started from October 1985. The minimum of 'large denomination deposits' which are exempted from the interest rate guidelines was reduced gradually from the original 1 billion yen to 500 million, 300 million and finally to 100 million yen (approx 800 thousand dollars) by April 1987, with maturity range of one month to two years.

Deregulation of small denomination deposits is rather complicated. When discussing the small-sized deposits, postal savings deposits, which amount to one third of total deposits held by individuals, cannot be ignored. Postal savings deposits are small deposits of 3 million yen or less at postal offices all over Japan. Before deregulating interest rates on small denomination bank deposits, it is necessary to work out an appropriate arrangement in order to ensure co-ordinated determination of interest rates on bank deposits and postal savings

[4] A. Viner, *Inside Japan's Financial Markets* (Tokyo, 1987) pp 145–185.

deposits. However, this has been politically rather difficult and the subject of major complaint by commercial banks. The ministries concerned are required to examine carefully the impact on the banks and the financial system in general and try to prevent any unwelcome or disorderly situation from arising.

SHORT-TERM MONEY MARKET

At the end of March 1987, the size of the Tokyo yen money markets has grown to around 90 trillion yen (approx 700 billion dollars), which includes interbank call money, bills discounted, yen swap, short-term government bonds, CD's and repurchase agreement of long-term bonds (*gensaki*). The size of the short-term money market has expanded very rapidly during recent years, now accounting for 27% of the GNP. Efforts have been made to encourage such development in the money market.

In June 1984, limitations on swap transactions of banks were removed and banks can now freely bring in foreign currency and convert it into yen for domestic use. This measure not only helped to supplement the yen money market, but also facilitated interest rate arbitrage between the domestic yen money market and the Euro-yen market. Banks can resort either to the traditional call, bills discount market or swap transactions, whichever offers lower interest cost.

The yen bankers acceptance market was established in Tokyo in June 1985. Japan's trade finance had been almost entirely dependent on dollar financing through the United States Bank Acceptance (BA's) market, except in the case of exports denominated in yen. Therefore, a new market for yen financing of trade was established in Japan and thereby offered a new money market for yen investment. The market so far has not grown much, mainly because exporters and importers have no difficulty in obtaining low-cost financing in other markets under current easy monetary conditions. The future development of this market remains to be seen.

Potentially the most important money market is that of short-term government debt of treasury bonds (TB's) which is quite new in Japan. Maturities of Japanese government bonds used to be from 2 to 20 years, with the bulk of issue in ten years. From fiscal year 1985, however, the refunding requirements of outstanding debt were quite large, ten years from the first large deficit financing in 1975. In order to facilitate the smooth refunding of such maturing bonds, the Japanese government decided to issue short-term government debt with the maturity of six months or less. The first such issue took place in February 1986. This move was welcomed by the market and the volume outstanding is increasing rapidly. In the near future, the short-term government debt market is expected to become one of the main short-term money markets in Japan, where banks and other large investors, domestic and foreign, adjust their liquidity positions and the Bank of Japan operates its monetary policy by selling and buying in the market.

More recently, a commercial paper market was established in Japan. Commercial paper (CP's) provides business corporations with timely and efficient means of financing and at the same time offers attractive yen investment instruments in the market. It takes the form of a promissory note issued by top-graded corporations, with minimum denominations of 100 million yen and maturities of one to six months, handled by both banks and securities houses, and in most cases supported by bank back-up facilities. The new commercial paper market is expected to diversify and increase the depth of the short-term yen market.

Finally, the recent development of the futures market in Japan should be mentioned. The futures market for Japanese government bonds has developed in the Tokyo Stock Exchange since October 1985, where both banks and securities houses actively participate in daily trading. The London International Financial Futures Exchange (LIFFE) listed the futures of the Japanese government bond in July 1987, which have been traded very successfully. Equity futures trading started in the Osaka Stock Exchange in June 1987 and the Tokyo Stock Exchange is contemplating the introduction of equity futures in 1988.

REVIEW OF THE EXISTING INSTITUTIONAL SYSTEM

Japan's Securities and Exchange Law prohibits financial institutions other than the licensed securities houses from engaging in securities business, similar to the regulation in the United States under the Glass-Steagall Act, although public bonds are excepted from this regulation. Also, Japan has adopted the so-called specialized banking system under which banks are divided into various groups and, in particular, long-term credit and short-term commercial banking services are separated and provided by different groups of banks.

This institutional framework was established after the Second World War and has functioned well, together with interest rate regulations and other guidelines, in maintaining a stable financial system and effectively channelling limited fund resources to the proper sectors during the period of rapid economic growth. However, as various markets are deregulated and funds flow freely from one market to another, such institutional rigidities have become difficult to maintain.

In order to facilitate expansion of the government bond market, banks were allowed to sell government bonds to their customers since 1983, and also to engage in dealing in government bonds from 1984. Securities companies were allowed, in turn, to sell new types of trust funds, mainly invested in medium-term government bonds and earning large returns, while highly liquid because they were cashable anytime after one month. They are said to have attracted a considerable sum of investors' money from bank deposits.

Arrangements have also been made so that the new money market instruments such as CD's, BA's and CP's are dealt with both by banks and securities houses. Thus, business areas where both banks and securities houses can operate have been expanding, while the core areas are left as they have been to banks and securities companies respectively.

As regards the division of long-term and short-term banking, the city banks which were primarily involved in commercial banking business now also engage

---

[5] Viner, supra, pp 22–27.

in long-term loans although their funding source is limited to deposits of two years or less maturity. They can avoid the risk of interest rate fluctuations arising from such mismatching of maturities by rolling-over short-term loans or applying floating interest rates. As long-term loans with floating interest rates become more popular, the division of long-term and short-term banking becomes obscure, although fixed interest rate loans extended by the long-term credit banks and funded by bank debentures will remain competitive.

The future of the specialized banking system has been on the agenda for discussion by the Advisory Committee to the Finance Minister since October 1985. A summary of discussions was made public by the end of 1987.

3. Access of foreign financial institutions to the Tokyo market

Another significant aspect of internationalization is access of foreign financial institutions to the Japanese market. Substantial progress has been made in this regard during the last three years.

First, concerning the Tokyo Stock Exchange (TSE) membership, the Exchange decided, in December 1985, to increase membership from 83 to 93, which provided opportunities for six foreign securities companies to become members. The TSE increased its membership again from 93 to 114 in November 1987, as it expanded computerized trading, and sixteen additional foreign companies were admitted as new members.

Secondly, securities licenses have been granted quite liberally to all eligible foreign applicants after normal processing of applications. Although the Japanese law prohibits banks from engaging in securities business, a practical solution is being sought on a case-by-case approach to allow a branch of a foreign bank's subsidiary to engage in securities business in Japan, if the parent bank holds 50% or less of the share of the subsidiary. Japan has gone even so far as to grant securities licenses to the subsidiaries of US commercial banks, while the US authorities are not as liberal because of the Glass-Steagall Act.

Thirdly, investment advisory and management services are now regulated under the new law enacted in May 1986. Companies must either register when engaging in advisory services or obtain licenses when managing discretionary accounts for customers. In accepting registration or granting licenses, all applications, domestic or foreign, were handled equitably and open-mindedly with much satisfaction from all applicants.

There are other areas in which progress has also been made such as trust banking licenses, where all nine foreign applications were fully accepted. All in all, the Japanese government's basic attitude is to welcome new entries of foreign financial institutions in the Tokyo market, hoping that they will help further develop and internationalize the Japanese market.

4. Internationalization of the yen

Internationalization of the yen denotes that the yen is to be used by foreigners in commercial and financial transactions. The yen is playing a greater role in financial transactions particularly in international bond issue and international lending, which accounts for 10% and 15% respectively of all currencies total last year. Foreign monetary authorities now have about 8% of their foreign exchange reserves in the yen.

Whether or not a currency should be allowed to be internationalized has been a subject of serious discussion among monetary authorities of major countries. These discussions indicate that difficult problems may arise as a result of internationalization of a particular currency. The foreign exchange market may become unstable because the currency will be traded not only in the domestic market but in foreign markets as well and consequently, subject to much more speculative transactions. The domestic monetary policy may not work as effectively as before, because in- and out-flow of funds will increase difficulties of controlling money supplies and interest rates. The domestic financial market may become disorderly because monetary policy will not be as effective as before and existing institutional systems may undergo a substantial change. In fact, countries other than the United States, including Germany and Switzerland all have reservations for greater internationalization of their own currencies.

The Advisory Committee to the Finance Minister has been consulted as to whether or not Japan should proceed with further internationalization of the yen. The Committee submitted a report in March 1985. It pointed out, *inter alia*, that the internationalization of the yen will develop inevitably, commensurate to the Japanese economic status in the world economy, and it is to the benefit of the Japanese economy. The Report recommended that restrictions should be removed and a favourable environment should be created to allow natural development of the international use of the yen in response to domestic as well as foreign needs. It also indicated that the internationalization of the yen may increase the scope of the foreign exchange market by permitting varieties of people to participate, thus having a stabilizing effect, as long as Japan's economic fundamentals are kept in good shape. It is true, according to the Report, that in order for the monetary policy to be effective, future development of the money market is particularly important. On the other hand, in order to minimize any unfavourable impact on the domestic financial systems, it was recommended to proceed gradually, hand-in-hand with liberalization of domestic financial markets.

There are two important areas in the internationalization of the yen; the Euro-yen market and the Tokyo offshore market.

EURO-YEN MARKET

In the Euro-market, international transactions are most actively carried on. The market will play an especially significant role in the internationalization of the yen.

Admittedly, the Euro-market is not without problems. It is beyond the control of any supervisory authorities, and the last resort is not there when credit crunch ever happens. The Euro-market, however, effectively matches lenders and borrowers of funds and connects national markets, and thus contributes to efficient capital movement. The Advisory Committee, therefore, officially acknowledged the indispensable role of the Euro-market.

Euro-yen transactions have been to a great extent deregulated. Qualified residents and non-residents are allowed to issue Euro-yen bonds. Non-residents can freely borrow Euro-yen, either long-term or short-term. Banks located abroad can issue Euro-yen CD's.

The second area which is important for the internationalization of the yen is the Tokyo offshore market, which opened in December 1986. It was a considerable success with the volume outstanding now exceeding 120 billion dollars. The market is intended to facilitate international transactions by providing the participants with special advantages which are not available in the domestic market.

The basic arrangements for the Tokyo offshore market are exemptions from interest rate regulations, reserve requirements and withholding tax on interest payments on deposits. In order to allow such exemptions, transactions must be made only with non-residents, that is, an out-out rule must be maintained. The offshore accounts are thus organised to take deposits only from non-residents and lend money only to non-residents.

The significance of the Tokyo offshore market can be summarized as follows. First, in the light of Tokyo's geographical location covering a time zone uncovered by London or New York markets and serving the Asian region which is experiencing a high rate of economic growth, the Tokyo offshore market is expected to perform the role of another international financial centre and as such help strengthen the world financial system. Secondly, it will act as a world centre for yen transactions and thus encourage further internationalization of the yen. Thirdly, it provides increased business opportunities, particularly for foreign financial institutions in Japan, through expansion of non-resident transactions. Japanese financial institutions will also benefit, by being able to reduce expenses involved in their international operations, if they are to be conducted in Tokyo.

5. Conclusion

As discussed so far, deregulation and internationalization of the Japanese financial markets is proceeding in a broad scope and steadily in a step-by-step manner.

Since deregulation means greater competition, sound management of the financial institutions becomes all the more important in the new financial environment. Under severe competition, mismanagement would easily result in business failure. Therefore, the Japanese government has been taking action to improve its supervisory functions for maintaining sound banking practices.

Capital adequacy and liquidity control are the important areas of attention. The Ministry of Finance is also reviewing the policy and methods of bank inspection, so that it can be an effective means for finding out potential difficulties the bank may face, and bring them to the management's attention as soon as possible. The deposit insurance system has also been enlarged and improved, so that bank failures, if any, would not result in a collapse of the whole financial system.

As regulating authorities of other countries are confronted with similar problems and therefore introduce new rules and guidelines, international co-operation and harmonization of financial supervision have gained significance. Since financial markets become more and more integrated, a failure in one market inevitably affects other markets. Foreign financial institutions also ask for a 'level playing field' with their domestic counterparts. Efforts have been made, therefore, to increase co-operation between regulatory authorities and work out common rules for bank supervision.

Japan is now expected to perform an active role in fostering sound development of international financial markets and thus facilitating smooth and efficient international flow of funds in order to realize better allocation of resources in the world economy. It is not known how long Japan may continue to have a large current account surplus and to function as a capital-exporting country. However, Japan may probably contribute to such smooth channelling of funds, regardless of its external position, by establishing an efficient and sound international capital market in the centre of the increasingly important Pacific Basin.

Progress of Financial and Capital Market Liberalization

Measures	Schedule (Time)	Current State and Future Prospect (Jun.1987)
A. Capital Market Liberalization		
1. Seek to remove interest rate ceilings on large denomination time deposits	Oct. 1 (1 billion and over / 2 years and less) → Apr. 1 1986 (500 million and over / 2 years and less) → Sep. 1 (300 million and over 2 years and less) → Apr. 6 1987 (200 million and over 2 years and less)	The minimum maturity will be shortened to one month in October, 1987
2. Introduction and deregulation of deposit instruments with market determined interest rates (MMCs)		
(1) Seek to lower the minimum de-nomination of MMCs	Sep. 1 (50 million → 30 million) → Apr. 6 1987 (30 million → 20 million)	Lowered the minimum denomination to ¥10 million in October, 1987
(2) Seek to enlarge further the ceiling on each bank's MMC issues	Jan.16 (Announced a concrete scheme on the instruments) Mar. 1 (Introduced) Oct. 1 (75%→150% of each bank's net worth) → Apr. 1 1986 (150%→200% of each bank's net worth) → Sep. 1 (200%→250% of each bank's net worth) → Apr. 6 1987 (250%→300% of each bank's net worth; as for foreign banks, the ceiling was removed)	The limit will be removed in October, 1987
(3) Seek to relax restrictions on the maturity of MMCs	Apr. 1 (extended from 6 months to 1 year) Apr. 6 (extended from 1year to 2year)	
(4) Seek to modify the interest rate ceiling of MMCs	Mar. 1 (CD-0.75%) Apr. 6 (with maturity of 1year and under CD-0.75% over 1year CD-0.5%)	
3. Ease guidelines on CDs		
(1) Seek to lower the minimum denomination of CDs	Jan. ○ (¥500million→¥300million) — Apr. ○ (¥300million→¥100million)	

Measures	Time / Schedule (1984–1987)	Current State and Future Prospect (Jun. 1987)
(2) Seek to enlarge further the ceiling on each bank's CD issues	1984 Apr. ○ (gradual enlargement) — 1985 Jun. ○ (100%→150% of each bank's net worth) Oct.1 — 1986 Apr.1 ○ (150%→200% of each bank's net worth) Sep.1 ○ (200%→250% of each bank's net worth) — 1987 Apr.6 ○ (250%→300% of each bank's net worth for foreign banks the ceiling was removed)	The limit will be removed in October, 1987
(3) Seek to relax restrictions on the maturity of CDs	Apr.1 ○ (Shortening of minimum maturity from 3 months to 1 month) 1986 Apr.1 ○ (extension of the maximum maturity from 6 months to 1 year)	We will study the possible problems accompanying and arising from it at early opportunity and we will promote it following liberalization of interest rate ceiling on large ones on the condition that the necessary circumstances are well established taking into account the protection of depositors, and the total balance between private bank deposits and postal savings, etc.
4. Liberalization of interest rate ceilings on small denomination deposits	Oct. ○ (start of study) May.22 ○ (report by Study Group on Financial Problems)	
5. Establish a yen-denominated banker's acceptance market	Jun.6 ○ (report by Committee on Financial System Research) — Dec.20 ○ (establishment of a concrete scheme of the market) — 1986 Jun.1 ○ (the start of the market) Apr.1 ○ (the start of the dealing by securities companies) — 1987 May.11 ○ (extension of the maturity 6months→1year lowered the minimum denomination 100million yen→50million yen)	
6. Short-term government debt issue	Feb.20 ○ (first issue of Treasury Bills)	The minimum denomination of TBs and FBs will be lowered from ¥100 million to ¥50 million by this August. As for TBs and FBs purchased by sovereign tax-exempt entities such as foreign central banks, a system under which the tax withheld at the time of purchase instead of the current treatment of refunding at the time of redemption will be introduced no later than this summer.
7. Eliminate the real demand rule in forward exchange transactions	1984 Apr.1 ○	Completed.
8. Remove the limits on oversold spot foreign exchange positions of banks	Jun.1 ○	Completed.

Measures	Time / Schedule (1984 – 1987)	Current State and Future Prospect (Jun. 1987)
10. Remove nonprudential restrictions on overseas yen lending from Japan by banks	1984 Apr. ○	Completed.
11. Permit qualified foreign banks to deal in already issued public bonds	Oct. 19 ○ (licensed three qualified foreign banks); May. 31 (licensed five qualified foreign banks); May. 30 ○ (licensed one qualified foreign banks); June 30 ○ (licensed two qualified foreign banks); May 29 ○ (licensed three qualified foreign banks)	
B. Access of Foreign Institutions to Japanese Money and Capital Markets		
1. Requested the Tokyo Stock Exchange to study ways of providing opportunities of membership to for-eign and domestic non-member firms, including the revision of the existing system	Feb. 1 (6 foreign companies were granted membership of the T.S.E.)	The Tokyo Stock Exchange is preparing to increase the number of its membership so that the new member can be determined by the end of this year.
2. License qualified foreign banks to participate in the trust banking activities	Dec. 20 ○ (announced the precise form of the participation and the criteria for selecting qualified banks); June 22 ○ (announced the list of eligible banks) (licensed nine eligible foreign banks)	Announced the list of eligible banks on 22 June 1985. (Nine foreign banks have started trust business)
3. Continue to promote transparency		Continue to promote transparency on entry and operation of foreign branches in Japan's capital markets.
C. Development of a Euroyen Invest ment and Banking Market		

Measures	Time / Schedule	Current State and Future Prospect (Jun. 1987)
1. Develop a Euroyen bond market		
(1) Ease guidelines on Euroyen bond issues by non-Japanese residents.		
① Expand the scope of non-resident issuers to include private corporations, local governments, etc.	Dec. 1 (1984)	Eased the guidelines on 1 December, 1984. The Advisory Committee submitted a recommendation to the Minister of Finance on 5 March 1985 to further liberalize guidelines on Euroyen bond issues by non-Japanese residents. Further relaxed the qualification standards for non-Japanese residents from 1 April, 1985.
②(i) Relax the qualification standards for non-resident private corporations	Dec. 1 (Introduced the qualification standards) / Apr. 1 (relaxed) / Apr. 1 (fully introduced the credit rating system)	Fully introduced the credit rating system in the qualification standards and added NIS, JCR and JBRI as the recognized rating agencies on 1 April, 1986
(ii) Expand the scope of the recognized rating agencies	Apr. 1 (expanded) / Jul. (added)	Fitch will be additionally recognized as the recognized rating agency in July, 1987
③ Remove the restrictions on the number and size of issues	Dec. 1	
④ New features	Jun. 17 (introduced new features) / Jun.	In line with the above recommendation introduced new features of Euroyen bonds from 17 June, 1986. Introduced four year Euroyen bond from June, 1987
⑤ Remove the restrictions on Euroyen bond issues by foreign banks	June 1	Admitted foreign banks, from 1 June, 1986, to issue Euroyen bond provided that they will not bring back to Japan the proceeds from their Euroyen bond issues.
(2) Ease guidelines on Euroyen bond issues by residents		The Advisory Committee submitted a recommendation to the Minister of Finance on 5 March, 1985 to further liberalize guidelines on Euroyen bond issues by residents
① Relax the qualification standards	Apr. 1 (1984) / Jul. (relaxed) / Oct. (relaxed) / Feb. (relaxed) / Jul.	In line with the above recommendation, relaxed the qualification standards for Euroyen bonds issued by residents in July, 1985 and in October, 1985 and in February, 1987, at the same time as the relaxation of domestic non-secured bonds. The credit rating system will be introduced in July, 1987
② New features	Jun. 17 (introduced new feature) / Apr. 1 (introduced new feature) / Jun.	Introduced dual currency bonds from June, 1985. Introduced floating rate notes and currency conversion bonds from 1 April, 1986 Introduced four year Euroyen bond from June, 1987

— 4 —

Measures	1984 Apr.	Jun.	1985 Jan.	Apr.	Jun.	1986 Jan.	Apr.	Jun.	Sep.	1987 Jan.	Apr.	Current State and Future Prospect (Jun. 1987)
(3) Shorten the seasoning period							Apr. 1 ○ (shortened)				→	Shortened the seasoning period from 180 days to 90 days on 1 April, 1986 except dual currency bonds.
(4) Remove restrictions on the lead and co-lead management of the issue of Euroyen bonds			Dec. 1 ○								→	Completed
(5) Expedite a study between Japanese and U.S. tax and financial officials with the aim of finding an appropriate solution on the problem of the withholding tax on interest earnings by non residents on Euroyen bonds issued by Japanese residents			Jan. 10 ○ (decided to remove)	Apr. 1. ○ (removed)								Removed on 1 April, 1985.
2. Authorize banks to issue short-term (6 months or less) Euroyen CDs sold outside of Japan			by the end of 1984 ○				Apr. 1 ○ (extended)				→	Implemented from 1 December, 1984. The Advisory Committee submitted a recommendation to the Minister of Finance on 5 March, 1985 to liberalize the issue of medium-and long-term Euroyen CDs. The maximum maturity of Euroyen CDs was extended up to one year on 1 April, 1986. (A.P)
3. Liberalize Euroyen lending												
(1) Liberalize Euroyen lending with maturities of one year or less	Jun. 1 ○										→	Completed
(2) Liberalize Euroyen lending with a maturity in excess of one year				Apr. 1 ○ (to non - residents)							→	The Advisory Committee submitted a recommendation to the Minister of Finance on 5 March, 1985 to liberalize medium-and long-term Euroyen lending. Liberalized Euroyen lending with a maturity in excess of one year to non-residents.
D. Direct Investment												
Reform the law to eliminate the designated company system	May. 18 ○ (the bill was passed by the Diet) Jul. 1 ○ (enforced)										→	Completed

Financial transactions in Japanese law

Masabumi Yamane
General Manager
Legal Department
The Bank of Tokyo, Ltd

1. Financial institutions

The primary role and function of financial institutions in Japan is the interme-
diation of credit and finance. There are several types of financial institutions in
Japan: some of them are called 'banks' while others are not. The most
significant of them are as follows:[1]

(1) Government banks:

(a) The Bank of Japan is the central bank of Japan and is the only bank which
is authorized to issue bank notes and coins. The Bank of Japan was
established pursuant to the Law of Bank of Japan (Law No 67, 24 February
1942).

(b) The Export and Import Bank of Japan, which was established pursuant to
the Law of Export Import Bank of Japan (Law No 268, 15 December 1950),
and The Development Bank of Japan, which was established pursuant to
the Law of the Development Bank of Japan (Law No 108, 31 March 1951),
are government banks which were founded for the purpose of implementing
the purposes described in Article 1 of their respective statutes.

(2) Commercial banks (*shougyou ginkou*):

Large commercial banks which are national in scope, ie 'all-nation banks'
(*zenkoku ginkou*), are divided into four categories: ordinary Banks (*futsuu
ginkou*), the foreign exchange bank (*gaikoku kawase ginkou*), long-term credit
banks (*chouki shinyou ginkou*) and trust banks (*shintaku ginkou*).

(i) Ordinary banks are banks which are established pursuant to the Banking

---

[1] J. Horne, *Japanese Financial Markets: Conflict and Consensus in Policymaking* (Sydney, Boston,
London, 1987) pp 28–34.

Law (Law No 59, 1 June 1981), successor to the old banking law (Law No 21, 30 March 1927). Twelve ordinary banks are city banks and another 64 are regional banks. The city banks (*toshi ginkou*) are urban-based banks. As previously noted, 12 ordinary banks are city banks. In addition, the Bank of Tokyo Ltd, which is a foreign exchange bank, is also considered to be a city bank. Ordinary banks also include 64 local banks (*chihou ginkou*) but their main business is limited to a local area, while the business of the city banks is nationwide.

(ii) The sole foreign exchange bank—the Bank of Tokyo Ltd—was established pursuant to the Law of Foreign Exchange Bank (Law No 67, 10 April 1954) for the purposes of engaging in foreign exchange business and facilitating foreign trade with Japan. It is not a bank under the Banking Law, but it is treated as an ordinary bank in many cases. All Japanese Banks (including the Foreign Exchange Bank) are subject to the provisions of the Foreign Exchange and Foreign Trade Control Law and the regulations thereunder.[2] Historically, however, the Ministry of Finance has treated the Foreign Exchange Bank more favorably than other financial institutions in terms of granting necessary approvals and providing government consents required by the provisions of the Foreign Exchange and Foreign Trade Control Law. This more favorable treatment takes into account the special nature of foreign exchange transactions.

(iii) Long-term credit banks are banks which were established pursuant to the Law of Long-Term Credit Bank (Law No 187, 12 June 1952) for the purpose of implementing long-term finance in Japan. There are, at present, three long-term credit banks (ie The Industrial Bank of Japan Ltd, The Long-Term Credit Bank of Japan Ltd and the Nippon Credit Bank Ltd). A long-term credit bank is neither a bank under the Banking Law, but it is in many cases treated as an ordinary bank. The foreign exchange bank and the long-term credit banks are authorized to issue bonds (*saiken*) in accordance with and pursuant to their respective statutes.

(iv) Trust banks are established pursuant to the Banking Law but are authorized to do trust business by the appropriate Minister (ie the Minister of Finance), pursuant to the Law relating to the combination, etc of trust business of Ordinary Banks (Law No 43, 11 March 1943). There are seven trust banks in Japan. The Trust Business Law (Law No 65, 21 April 1921) provides that no person may engage in trust business unless authorized to do so by the appropriate Minister. At present, except for these seven banks and one ordinary bank which has also been authorized to do trust business, no financial institutions (other than two local banks in Okinawa) are entitled to do such business in Japan.

Small and medium sized financial institutions are divided into three categories: (i) mutual banks (*sougo ginkou*), which were established pursuant to the Law of Mutual Bank (Law No 199, 5 June 1951), (ii) credit associations (*shinyou*

---

[2] A. D. Smith, 'The Japanese Foreign Exchange and Foreign Trade Control Law and Administrative Guidance: the Labyrinth and the Castle', *Law and Policy in International Business* (vol 16, 1984) pp 440–456.

kinko), which were established pursuant to the Law of the Credit Association (Law No 238, 15 June 1951) and (iii) credit co-operative unions (*shinyou kyoudou kumiai*), which were established pursuant to the Law of the Co-operative Union for small to medium sized enterprises, etc (Law No 181, 1 June 1949).

While some other financial institutions exist in Japan, such institutions are beyond the scope of this paper.

2. Banking business

Financial institutions are not regulated by a single and unitary law, but by several independent and separate laws. The most significant of them is the Banking Law (Law No 59, 1981).[3] In the course of doing business, a bank is required to work in the interest of the public as well as to gain profit for its own behalf. Such a mandate makes it necessary to define the outline of banking business, so that a bank may maintain its healthy operation.

The scope of Japanese banking business is stipulated in Articles 10 to 12 of the Banking Law as follows:

(a) A bank may engage in the following activities: (i) accepting deposits and instalment savings (instalment savings means accepting deposits which are made at several times, either as fixed instalments or within a fixed period, and making payments of an agreed sum at a fixed time), (ii) to make loans and to discount bills (bills of exchange) or notes (promissory notes) and (iii) to do exchange transactions (Art 10, s 1). These kinds of business are deemed to be 'proper banking business' for a bank under the Banking Law.

(b) A bank may engage in the following business or other business ancillary to its banking business:

  (i) to guarantee liabilities or to accept bills;
 (ii) to buy or sell securities (which are made for a bank's own portfolio investment or for the account of a bank's customers at the written request of such customers);
(iii) to lend securities;
(iv) to underwrite government bonds, local government bonds, and bonds guaranteed by the government (collectively 'Government Bonds'), for purposes other than selling or offering subscriptions for such government bonds;
 (v) to acquire or to assign monetary claims (including negotiable certificates of deposit and such other claims as are embodied in instruments designated by an Ordinance of the Ministry of Finance);
(vi) to act as a subscription agency for local government bonds or corporate bonds or other bonds;

---

[3] As for the new Banking Law, see B. W. Semkow, 'Japanese Banking Law: Current Deregulation and Liberalization of Domestic and External Financial Transaction', *Law and Policy in International Business* (1985, No 1) p 81ff.

(vii) to act as an agent for banks and other financial institutions (which are designated by an Ordinance of the Ministry of Finance);

(viii) to receive, pay and conduct other monetary operations on behalf of the government, or local governments, public bodies, corporations, etc;

(ix) to safekeep securities, precious metals and other articles; and

(x) money changing (Art 10, s 2).

(c) A bank may, in addition to the banking business set forth in (a) and (b) above, and provided that performance of the business set forth in (a) above shall not be precluded thereby, engage in the business of underwriting, offering for subscription or sale , buying, selling and/or otherwise dealing in government bonds, etc (Art 11).

(d) Further, a bank may not engage in any business other than (1) that set forth in (a), (b) and (c) of the above-mentioned provisions and (2) business allowed by the Law of Trust for Secured Bonds (Law No 52, 13 March 1905) and any other law (Art 12).

(e) Notification of the Director of the Banking Bureau, MOF (*Kuragin* No 1968 of 3 July 1975, as amended) of the Ministry of Finance under the title of 'Re: The Relationship Between Financial Institutions and their Related Companies' stipulates that (i) credit guarantee business, (ii) factoring business, (iii) credit card business (those businesses described in (i), (ii) and (iii) are deemed to be permitted by the s 10.02 of the Banking Law and referred to as 'Other Ancillary Business' (*sonota fuzui gyoumu*)), and (iv) mortgage instrument business (*teitou shouken*) are businesses which a bank may engage in through related companies. A bank may not engage in mortgage instrument business as its own business. This Notification further stipulates that a bank is additionally entitled to have its related companies engage in leasing business, venture capital business, management consulting business and others (for the purposes of this Notification, 'related company' means a company in which a bank has an equity interest and with which a bank has a deep and close relationship, particularly with respect to creation, capital relationship and personal (ie management) relationship).

Notwithstanding the limitations outlined above, a bank may conduct through its wholly-owned subsidiaries agency activities for the benefit of other financial institutions and certain activities (such as operational services for its own office buildings and welfare services for its own employees) which are not basic banking activities but are necessary in the course of doing business.

Those businesses that a bank may engage in through its related companies are referred to as 'Fringe Business' (*shuhen gyoumu*). As stated above, banking business is composed of (i) the proper business, (ii) the ancillary business, (iii) the other ancillary business and (iv) the fringe business.

3. Statutory restrictions on bank transactions

(1) Article 65 of the Securities and Exchange Law (Law No 25, 1948) (*shouken torihiki hou*) prohibits financial institutions from engaging in any aspect of the securities business (*shoukengyo*), with some exceptions (as defined in Article 2 of the Securities and Exchange Law). Therefore, a bank may not engage in securities business, except when such business is allowed by Article 11 of the Banking Law.[4]

It is understood that the business permitted pursuant to Article 11 of the Banking Law is not deemed to be securities business. Accordingly, the provisions of the Securities and Exchange Law are not applied to such business. Currently, it is a difficult matter to determine where the 'fence' that separates the scope of banking business from the scope of securities business shall be removed or not. A bank is required to obtain permission from the Minister of Finance when it intends to engage in the business described in Article 11 of the Banking Law. Although Article 65 of the Security and Exchange Law prohibits banks, trust banks and other financial institutions from engaging in certain securities related business described therein, the Law does not prohibit such financial institutions from engaging in such securities-related business indirectly through offshore subsidiaries established for the specific purpose of doing securities-business outside Japan. Such subsidiaries are referred to as 'overseas security subsidiaries' (*kaigai shouken genchihoujin*).

In order to reconcile securities companies and the banks, as a guideline, three bureaux of the Ministry of Finance (eg, Banking Division, Security Division and International Finance Division) have reached an agreement, the so-called 'Three Bureaux Agreement' (*sankyoku shidou*). The three Bureaux agreed that decisions regarding the establishment of overseas security subsidiaries by Japanese banks and the authorization of the appointment to lead manager status of such overseas security subsidiaries for the purpose of overseas bond issues should be controlled by the government. It should be determined only after taking into account the past experiences and roles of such Japanese banks as well as the purposes of Article 65 of the Securities and Exchange Law. This Three Bureaux Agreement is interpreted by banking and securities circles in a different way. The banks are inclined to understand that their overseas security subsidiaries can, to a certain extent, be freely appointed as lead managers in respect of foreign bond issues. Securities circles, however, have a different view.

(2) The Interest Limitation Law (Law No 100, 1954) (*risoku seigen hou*) stipulates that the highest interest rate payable in respect of borrowed funds shall not exceed certain fixed rates, and that any agreement to pay interest exceeding such rates shall be deemed to be null and void. There is little doubt that this law will be applied to the interest rate applicable to cross border banking transactions without any further consideration. The Temporary Interest Control Law (Law No 181, 1947) (*rinji kinri chousei hou*) stipulates that the Minister of Finance is entitled to determine, as he may think proper, the highest interest rate applicable to banking transactions with any financial institution. This law is not currently applied to foreign currency transactions. These two

---

[4] A. Viner, *Inside Japan's Financial Market* (Tokyo 1987) pp 22–27.

laws are enacted for the purpose of giving protection to customers of financial institutions.

(3)(a) Article 9 of the Law Relating to Prohibition of Private Monopoly and Preserving Fair Trade (Law No 54, 1947) (*shiteki dokusen no kinshi oyobi kousei torihiki no kakuho ni kansuru houritsu* or *dokkin hou*) stipulates that (i) no holding companies shall be established and (ii) no company shall become a holding company. For the purposes of this law, a holding company means 'a company the principal purpose of which is to control the business operations of another company in Japan by means of owning of stocks or other equitable interest'.[5]

(b) Article 11 of the Anti-Monopoly Law prohibits a financial institution from acquiring stock in excess of 5% of the issued and outstanding capital of a Japanese company unless such acquisition has otherwise been allowed by the Fair Trade Commission of Japan.

When a customer is required to make deposits with a bank and is not permitted by the bank to withdraw such deposits without instructions from the bank, such deposits are sometimes called 'Restrictive Deposits' (*kosokusei yokin*). Typical restrictive deposits are insurance deposits (*buzumi yokin*) and straddling deposits (*ryoudate yokin*). The former is a deposit with a bank to be made from a part of proceeds of discounted bills or notes, and the latter is a deposit with a bank to be made from a part of loan proceeds. A bank may not take advantage of a customer's weak bargaining position by requiring the customer to make a restrictive deposit whether by way of pledge or otherwise. It is generally acknowledged the bank's position is superior to that of its customers, particularly where the bank grants credit facilities to the customer. Granting a credit facility to a customer pursuant to which restrictive deposits are required is deemed to be an unfair trade practice under the Anti-Monopoly Law and is prohibited pursuant to Article 19 of the Law if such requirement is deemed to be in excess of necessary security purposes in connection with the granting such credit facility. Case law does not always deny the effectiveness of the restrictive deposit insofar as the actual rate of interest on the non-restricted proceeds of the loan would not exceed the highest rate provided for by any usuary law.[6] Restrictive deposits are also strictly regulated by a series of guidelines issued by the Ministry of Finance ordering banks to take certain self-disciplinary measures. Recently, however, there has been a tendency towards relaxed enforcement.

(4) Banking transactions are also subject to the restrictions stipulated in the Foreign Exchange and Foreign Trade Control Law (Law No 228, 1 December 1949, as amended) (*gaikoku kawase oyobi gaikoku boueki kanri hou*).

(5) Finally, banking transactions are subject to such regulations, orders and guidelines, as are issued by the government from time to time for administrative purposes. One of the most important guidelines presently in effect is a

---

[5] As for the Anti-Monopoly Law, see M. Nakagawa, *Anti-Monopoly Legislation in Japan* (Tokyo, 1984).
[6] Judgment of the Supreme Court, 20 June 1977 (*Minshū* 31-4-449: known as *Gifu Shinyou Kumiai* case).

regulation governing large loans issued by certain types of financial institutions. This is known as the 'big amount loan regulation' (ōguchi yūshi kisei). According to the 'big amount loan regulation' (kuragin 4481, 25 December 1974), lending limits of each bank to any single debtor are determined as follows:[7]

as to ordinary banks:	20% of the amount of its issued and paid-in capital plus reserves
as to trust banks:	30% of the amount of its issued and paid-in capital plus reserves
as to long-term credit banks:	30% of the amount of its issued and paid-in capital plus reserves
as to foreign exchange bank:	40% of the amount of its issued and paid-in capital plus reserves.

4. General terms and conditions of banking transactions

Printed contracts which are prepared in advance and which contain terms and conditions applicable to all potential customers are called 'Standard Agreements' (yakkan or futsū torihiki yakkan). Standard Agreements are broadly used in commercial transactions, particularly in the insurance business, transportation business and warehousing.

Standard Agreements are provided by one party to the contract in a printed form and the other contracting party is required to sign the printed form and return it to the party who prepared the form. It is generally understood that the party preparing the form of Standard Agreement is in a superior bargaining position and that the potential customer has no choice but to sign and agree to the standard form contract.

When a customer wishes to receive a credit facility from a bank, the customer is requested to sign a form of Agreement on Bank Transactions prepared by the bank, the terms and conditions of which apply to all potential transactions between a customer and a bank. The model form of Agreement on Bank Transactions prevailing at present was adopted and officially published by the National Association of Bankers (zenginkyou) on 19 April 1977. This form has been adopted as is or with minor alterations by all member banks. Similarly, the national association of Mutual Banks, Credit Associations and Credit Co-operative Unions have each adopted a model form of Agreement on Mutual Bank Transactions, Agreement on Credit Association Transactions and Agreement on Credit Co-operative Union Transactions respectively. The terms contained in these agreements are substantially identical to those contained in the Agreement on Bank Transactions, and each member mutual bank, credit association and credit co-operative union has adopted the relevant model form as proposed or with minor alteration.

Therefore, at present, all Japanese commercial banks and other financial

[7] Semkow, supra, p 116.

institutions have almost the same terms and conditions in respect of credit facilities transactions.

The National Association of Bankers has also officially published model forms of standard agreements relating to particular bank transactions, such as: the Agreement on Overdrafts in Current Account (*touza kanjyou kashikoshi keiyakusho*), Current Account Regulations (*touza kanjyo kitei*), the Agreement on Guarantee of Payment (*shiharai-shoudaku yakujyousho*), the Agreement on Purchase or Negotiation of Bills (*gaikokumuke kawase tegata torihiki yaku-jyousho*), the Agreement on Forward Foreign Exchange Contracts (*sakimono gaikoku kawase torihiki ni kansuru yakujyosho*), etc.

The basic Standard Agreements relating to deposit transactions are the model form of Agreement for Ordinary Deposit and the model form of Agreement for Current Deposit Account. The standard form agreement relating to credit facility transactions is the form of Agreement on Bank Transactions.

Various other Standard Agreements have been made based upon these basic Standard Agreements, the most important of which are: the Agreement on Overdraft in Current Account, the Agreement on Guarantee of Payment, the Agreement on Purchase or Negotiation of Bills, the Agreement on Forward Foreign Exchange Contracts, the Commercial Letter of Credit Agreement, and the Agreement on Submission of Negotiable Instruments as Security.

In Japan, each local region has a bankers' association. It is composed of the banks and branches of banks located in each such local region. These local bankers' associations in turn have established the National Association of Bankers. Presently the National Association is composed of 73 local bankers' associations. Other financial institutions have also established similar associations on a national basis, including the National Association of Credit Associations (*zenkoku shinyou kinko rengoukai*) and the National Association of Credit Co-operative Unions (*zenkoku shinyou kyoudou kumiai rengoukai*).

The purpose of the National Association of Bankers is to promote developments of the economy through banking business as well as by promoting mutual communication among the local bankers' associations. In particular, the rules of the National Association of Bankers specify the following goals: (i) to conduct research and study financial and economic matters and to propose initiatives in these areas to the government, (ii) to communicate and co-operate with other business organizations, and (iii) to discuss and propose methods for the improvement of the banking business.

Although the Japanese legal system belongs to the group of Continental Law countries and codification of its laws has developed, Japanese statutes relating to commercial transactions (including banking transactions) are not necessarily adequate to settle various contractual disputes. Therefore, it is essential for banks to protect their rights and claims against their customers by concluding agreements more favorable to the banks from their customers.

The Civil Code of Japan (Law No 89, 1896) and the Commercial Code of Japan (Law No 48, 1899) are the most important Japanese statutes governing commercial transactions, including banking performance. These statutes are broad in scope and were not enacted solely for the purpose of regulating banking transactions. As banking business is usually transacted in a uniform manner, it has generated many customs of trade, some of which were eventually recognized by statute or by the courts as case law.

The creation of standard forms of agreements containing common terms and conditions applicable equally to any banking transactions has contributed much to the development and expansion of banking activities in Japan. This effort has resulted in the elimination of individual negotiations with bank customers regarding the terms of each banking transaction and has also helped to minimize the risk which arises as a result of poorly drafted documentation.

Standard Agreements fix and standardize the terms of routine banking transactions and, in turn, enable a bank to do business with a great many customers at the same time. This is favorable to banking customers for the simplicity of business and low cost; however, the terms of Standard Agreements are not always favorable to banking customers, because they are obligated to accept the terms of standard agreements without any negotiation.

These Standard Agreements are usually submitted by the customer to a bank in the following manner: the customer signs and delivers to the bank the form of the relevant Standard Agreements. The bank will not countersign such forms, it just receives them and holds them in its vault. This practice is called the 'submission method' (*sashiire houshiki*). This practice is criticized on the grounds that: (i) as no agreement on the part of a bank is described in the Standard Agreements, the rights of the customer against the bank are not clear, and (ii) some of the terms and conditions contained in the Agreement on Bank Transactions are much too favorable to the bank.

It has been discussed for sometime how and why the terms and conditions contained in Standard Agreements are binding upon the customer upon signing such agreements without countersignature by the bank.

It is understood that, in order to bind the customer by the terms and conditions contained in such Standard Agreements, the customer should be shown the contents of the agreements in advance and that the agreement itself should be written in plain style and comprehensive in nature.

After the previous model form of Agreement on Bank Transactions had been adopted in 1962 by the National Association of Bankers, it was recognized that the standard form agreement was designed primarily to protect the rights of a bank against its customers and that the form should be altered to allow some protection to the customers of a bank.

In 1972, the National Life Council (*kokumin seikatsu shingikai*) published a report under the title 'Protection for Consumers in respect of Financial Services—Present Situation, Points of Contention and Future Directions'. In addition to this report, the Ministry of Finance suggested the insertion of a set off clause which would grant customers of a bank the right of set off against the bank, and the National Association of Bankers started work on altering the previous model form of Agreement on Bank Transactions.

In response to the Report, the National Association of Bankers officially published on 19 April 1977 a new model form of Agreement on Bank Transactions (which is prevailing up to this date). The new model form of Agreement on Bank Transactions altered the old model form, in particular by (i) acknowledging a set off by a customer against a bank, and (ii) altering the acceleration clause by changing the enumerated events of default.

It is generally understood that the terms and conditions contained in the Agreement on Bank Transactions and the related agreements submitted by a bank's customer in connection with the Agreement on Bank Transactions, are not strictly enforced so long as the relationship between the customer and the bank is generally good. Practically speaking, disputes or misunderstandings between a bank and its customers are settled through the custom of trade or mutually amicable discussions, regardless of the actual terms and conditions contained in the Agreement on Bank Transactions and the other related documents.

However, in the event that a dispute between a bank and its customer is brought to court, the standard form of Agreement on Bank Transactions would be material evidence upon which a court would rely in rendering its judgment. Because it is foreseen that a bank would win in any court action, customers generally refrain from bringing a dispute with a bank to court.

The Terms and conditions set forth in the form of Agreement on Bank Transactions adopted by The Bank of Tokyo Ltd (the 'Bank') is outlined as follows:

(a) Title and Recitals:

The Agreement on Bank Transactions is addressed to the Bank and is executed and delivered by the customer (and, when there is a guarantor, by the guarantor). The customer acknowledges that he agrees to the terms set forth below.

It is understood that a contract between a customer and the Bank is made when the Agreement on Bank Transactions is signed and delivered by the customer and duly accepted by the Bank. The conclusion of such contract does not create the Bank's obligation to lend or the customer's obligation to borrow. The actual contract granting a credit facility and the obligations created thereby are made by a separate agreement made in addition to the Agreement on Bank Transactions.

(b) Article 1 of the Agreement on Bank Transactions stipulates that the scope of banking transactions covered by the agreement is as follows:

(i) Loans against bills of exchange and promissory notes:
Short-term loans are usually made by the Bank to the borrower in exchange for the borrower's delivery of a short-term promissory note, which may be renewed or extended by replacement with a new promissory note having a maturity date of one year (for example) from the date of maturity of the old promissory note. Interest for the period from the date of issue to the maturity date is usually paid in advance on the date on which the loan is made or renewed.

(ii) Discounts of bills of exchange or promissory notes:
The Bank usually discounts promissory notes or bills of exchange issued by persons other than the borrower at a certain fixed discount rate. Legally, the discount itself is deemed to be a purchase of promissory notes or bills of exchange.

(iii) Loans by deed:
For medium and long-term loans (loans having a maturity of more than one year), the customer is required to sign and deliver an instrument of Credit Obligations (*kinsen shouhitaishaku keiyaku shousho*) prepared by the Bank. Such Instrument of Borrowing Obligations shall contain a description of each

term of borrowing (interest rate, principal amount, maturity, etc). Upon the Bank's receipt thereof, the Instrument of Borrowing Obligations constitutes a loan agreement between the Bank and the customer. In addition to the Instrument of Borrowing Obligations, the customer is sometimes required to deliver to the Bank a promissory note as security for the loan (*tegata heiyou shousho kashitsuke*). This is in contrast to the practice in the USA where loan agreements usually contain a provision in which the customer is required to deliver a promissory note to the lender as evidence of, rather than as security for, a loan.

(iv) Overdrafts:
For an overdraft facility, a customer is required to sign and deliver to the Bank an Agreement on Overdraft in Current Account (*touza kanjyou kashikoshi keiyakusho*) in the form prepared by the Bank.

(v) Acceptances and Guarantees:
When a customer requests the Bank to issue a guarantee in favor of a third-party creditor of the customer as security for the obligations of the customer or a certain other person to such third-party creditor, the customer is required to sign and deliver a Request for a Bank Guarantee and an Agreement on Guarantee of Payment, both in the form prepared by the Bank. One element of this agreement is the customer's indemnification of the Bank in respect of the Bank's payment of the guaranteed obligations. In some cases, the Bank is entitled to demand that a customer pay the amount of guaranteed obligations even prior to its payment of guaranteed obligations.

(vi) Foreign exchange:
There are several forms of agreement for foreign exchange transactions, the most important of which are the Agreement on Purchase or Negotiation of Bills and the Agreement on Forward Foreign Exchange Contracts.

(vii) Commercial Letter of Credit:
When a customer requests that the Bank issue a letter of credit, the customer is required to sign and deliver to the Bank the Commercial Letter of Credit Agreement.

(viii) Other transactions:
Certain other transactions, such as the lending of securities, are also covered by the Agreement on Bank Transactions.

(ix) In addition the Agreement on Bank Transactions governs transactions relating to promissory notes or bills of exchange which have been issued, endorsed, accepted, accepted by intervention or guaranteed by a customer and acquired by the Bank from a third party.

(c) Article 2 of the Agreement on Bank Transactions provides that the Bank is entitled to exercise all of its rights against a customer, whether those rights flow from the agreement itself or from the promissory notes or bills of exchange.

(d) Article 3 (1) stipulates that the Bank is entitled to change the rate of interest applicable to loans, etc, in cases where a material change in the financial situation has occurred (such as a change in the official rate), provided that the new interest rate is reasonable.

(e) Article 3 (2) provides for a penalty rate of 14.0% per annum (on a basis of a year of 365 days) on late payments. The Civil Code (Art 420) allows an agreement in respect of penalty interest in the case of payment default. In the case of ordinary interest, in the absence of an agreement between the bank and its customer, Article 514 of the Commercial Code of Japan sets a 6% per annum rate.

(f) Article 4 provides that the Bank may demand that a customer grant a security interest in its assets or those of a third person, or provide a guaranty in favor of the Bank when the Bank, in its reasonable discretion, deems it necessary. Article 4 thus constitutes a general security agreement by the customer to some extent, but sometimes, depending on the type of additional security obtained, it is necessary for the Bank to obtain a separate security or guaranty instrument.

(g) Article 5 stipulates that if one of the events of default set forth in Item 1 of Article 5 occurs, then any and all obligations of a customer to the Bank shall, without any notice from the Bank, become immediately due and payable. If one of the events of default listed in Item 2 of Article 5 occurs, then the Bank is entitled to declare, upon demand, that any and all of the obligations of the customer to the Bank are immediately due and payable in accordance with such demand. Historically, Article 5 has been very important to the Bank, particularly with respect to the Bank's right of set off, which is strictly regulated by the Civil Code of Japan. Article 137 of the Civil Code of Japan stipulates that a customer becomes unable to assert the 'benefit of time' defense in the event the customer has (i) been declared bankrupt, (ii) intentionally destroyed or diminished the security given, or (iii) failed to provide the creditor with the security the customer was obligated to furnish. Thus Article 5 is essential for the protection of the Bank, since Article 505 of the Civil Code of Japan allows set off only in cases where both claims are due.

After a long period of transition, recent case law[8] now allows banks to set off against a customer's deposits ahead of creditors who have provisionally attached such deposits, provided that the obligations to the bank had existed prior to such attachment. The importance of Article 5 has diminished to some extent, but it still brings the Bank various benefits.

(h) The Agreement on Bank Transactions contains various provisions relating to promissory notes or bills of exchange transactions; accordingly it may be said that it is a kind of an agreement of notes and bills.

(i) Furthermore, the Agreement on Bank Transactions contains provisions as to manner of set off, manner of appropriation of payment of moneys, applicable rate and time of currency exchange; and other similar matters.

---

[8] Judgment of the Supreme Court, 24 June 1970 (*Minshū* 24-6-587).

(j) Article 25 of the Code of Civil Procedures of Japan (Law No 29, 21 April 1890) stipulates that the parties concerned may choose or elect by mutual agreement a competent court in which to resolve their dispute (in cases other than appeals) and Article 14 of the Agreement on Bank Transactions stipulates that in the event of a dispute arising under the Agreement on Bank Transactions the parties shall submit to the jurisdiction of the court in the city in which the head office of the Bank or relevant branch office of the Bank is situated.

Appendix

AGREEMENT ON BANK TRANSACTIONS

TO: THE BANK OF TOKYO, LTD.

I/we do hereby agree to the terms and conditions set forth in the following Articles in regard to my/our transactions with your Bank:

Article 1-0   (Scope of Application)
   (1)   I/we shall abide by this Agreement pertaining to the performance of my/our obligations arising from loans against Bills of Exchange (hereinafter referred to as 'Bills') and Promissory Notes (hereinafter referred to as 'Notes'), discounts of Bills and Notes, loans by deed, overdrafts, acceptances and guarantees, foreign exchanges, letters of credit, and any and all other transactions.
   (2)   Even in cases in which your Bank has, through your Bank's transactions with any third party, acquired Bills and Notes drawn, endorsed, accepted, accepted by intervention, or guaranteed by me/us, I/we shall also abide by this Agreement pertaining to the performance of my/our obligations evidenced by such Bills and Notes.

Article 2   (Obligations in Bills and Notes and Money Borrowed)
   In cases in which your Bank has granted me/us loans accompanied by Bills and Notes, your Bank may demand from me/us the payment of my/our obligations arising from the loans by exercising your Bank's rights either on the Bills and Notes or on the loans.

Article 3   (Interest, Damages, etc.)
   (1)   In regard to the stipulations concerning the rates of interest, discount charges, guarantee fees, handling commissions and rebates of any thereof, and also concerning the time and method of payment thereof, I/we shall agree, in the event of changes in the financial situation or any other reasonable and probable causes arising, to the revision of the stipulations to those in the range prevailing generally.
   (2)   In case I/we fail to perform any obligations which I/we owe your Bank, I/we shall pay your Bank damages at the rate of 14% per annum for the amount payable. In this case the calculation will be made on the actual number of days on a 365-day year basis.

Article 4   (Security)
   (1)   In cases in which a reasonable and probable cause necessitates the preservation of your Bank's rights, I/we shall upon demand forthwith furnish to your Bank such security or additional security, or such guarantors or additional guarantors, as may be approved by your Bank.
   (2)   Any and all security which has been furnished and that to be furnished in the future to your Bank for specific obligations shall constitute security

that covers and secures not only such obligations, but also any and all other obligations which I/we at present or in the future may owe your Bank.

(3)　Your Bank may collect or dispose of security in the manner, at the time, and for the price, etc. generally deemed proper, not necessarily following the procedures prescribed by law, and deduct expenses from the proceeds and appropriate the remainder to the payment of my/our obligations regardless of the priority prescribed by law; and in the event any obligations still remain, I/we shall pay them forthwith.

(4)　In cases in which I/we fail to perform any obligations which I/we owe your Bank, your Bank may collect or dispose of my/our movables, Bills and Notes, and other instruments and securities in your Bank's possession; and in such cases, I/we shall agree to your Bank's handling the matter mutatis mutandis in the manner set forth in the preceding paragraph.

Article 5　(Acceleration of Payment)

(1)　In case any one of the following events occurs to me/us, any and all obligations I/we owe your Bank shall immediately become due and payable without any notice or demand, etc. from your Bank and; I/we shall pay such obligations forthwith:

1.　When I/we have become unable to pay debts or application or petition is submitted for bankruptcy, commencement of composition of creditors, commencement of corporate reorganization proceedings, commencement of company arrangement, or commencement of special liquidation.

2.　When the Clearing House in observance of its rules takes procedures for suspension of my/our transactions with banks and similar institutions.

3.　When order or notice of provisional attachment, preservative attachment or attachment is dispatched in respect of my/our or the guarantor's deposits and/or any other credits with your Bank.

4.　When my/our whereabouts become unknown to your Bank due to my/our failure to notify your Bank of change of my/our address or any other causes attributable to me/us.

(2)　In any of the following cases, upon your Bank's demand, any and all obligations I/we owe your Bank shall immediately become due and payable; and I/we shall pay them forthwith:

1.　When I/we fail to pay any of my/our obligations to your Bank when it is due.

2.　When property offered to your Bank as security is attached or public auction procedure is commenced in respect of such property.

3.　When I/we violate the stipulations of any transactions with your Bank.

4.　When the guarantor falls under any one of the items of the preceding Paragraph or this Paragraph.

5.　In addition to each of the preceding items, when a reasonable and probable cause necessitates the preservation of your Bank's rights.

Article 6　(Repurchase of Discounted Bills and Notes)

(1)　In cases in which I/we have had Bills and Notes discounted by your Bank and any one of the items in Paragraph (1) of the preceding Article occurs to me/us, then pertaining to all such Bills and Notes, or in cases in which the principal obligors of my/our discounted Bills and Notes fail to pay them on due dates or any one of the items in Paragraph (1) of the preceding Article occurs to the principal obligors, then pertaining to the Bills and Notes wherein such persons are the principal obligors, I/we shall assume as a matter of course the repurchasing obligations for the face value of my/our discounted Bills and Notes without any notice or demand, etc. from your Bank; and I/we shall pay them forthwith.

(2) In cases other than those provided for in the preceding Paragraph, in which a reasonable and probable cause necessitates the preservation of your Bank's rights pertaining to the Bills and Notes which your Bank has discounted, I/we shall assume, upon your Bank's demand, the repurchasing obligations for the face value of my/our discounted Bills and Notes; and I/we shall pay them forthwith.

(3) As long as I/we do not perform the obligations set forth in the preceding two Paragraphs, your Bank may exercise any and all rights as holder of the Bills and Notes.

Article 7   (Deductions in Accounts)

(1) In cases in which I/we must perform any obligations owed to your Bank because they become due or because of acceleration of payment or because I/we have assumed the repurchasing obligations or because your Bank has acquired the right of claiming compensation from me/us or for any other causes, your Bank may set off against any such obligations at any time any of my/our deposits and/or any other credits with your Bank irrespective of the due dates of such deposits and/or other credits.

(2) In cases in which your Bank is able to effect a setoff as mentioned in the preceding Paragraph, your Bank may also obtain withdrawals from my/our deposits in lieu of my/our doing so, and may appropriate any such withdrawals to payments of my/our obligations, omitting any advance notice and also not adhering to established procedures.

(3) In cases in which your Bank makes any deductions in accounts according to the provisions of the preceding two Paragraphs, interest on my/our credits and obligations, discount charges and damages, etc. shall be calculated up to the date on which the actual calculation is made by your Bank for the purpose of deductions, and the rate of interest and tariffs shall be in accordance with those fixed by your Bank; and with regard to the foreign exchange rate, the rate quoted at your Bank at the time when the actual calculation is made by your Bank shall apply.

Article 7-2   (Ditto)

(1) I/we may set off any obligations I/we owe your Bank against my/our deposits and/or any other credits with your Bank which have become due, even when such obligations have not yet become due.

(2) When I/we effect a setoff under the provision of the preceding Paragraph with regard to the Bills and Notes which your Bank has discounted and which have not yet become due, I/we may do so upon assuming the repurchasing obligations for the face value of the discounted Bills and Notes; provided, however, that I/we may not effect a setoff with regard to Bills and Notes which your Bank has discounted and assigned to a third party.

(3) With regard to my/our credits or obligations in foreign currency or in free yen, I/we may not, notwithstanding the provisions of the preceding two Paragraphs, effect a setoff until and unless they have become due and procedures required under foreign exchange laws and regulations have been completed for them.

(4) In cases in which I/we effect a setoff under the provisions of the preceding

three Paragraphs, a notice of the setoff shall be made in writing and I/we shall affix my/our seal impression or signature which has previously been filed with your Bank to the certificate or passbook representing my/our deposits and/or other credits with your Bank which I/we have set off against my/our obligations and submit the same to your Bank forthwith.

(5) In cases in which I/we effect a setoff, interest on my/our credits and obligations, discount charges and damages, etc. shall be calculated up to the date on which my/our notice of the setoff arrives at your Bank, and the rate of interest and tariffs shall be in accordance with those fixed by your Bank; and with regard to the foreign exchange rate, the rate quoted at your Bank at the time when the actual calculation is made by your Bank for the purpose of setoffs shall apply. If there is an agreement providing for special charges payable when obligations are paid prior to their due dates, I/we shall abide by such agreement.

Article 8 (Presentment and Delivery of Bills and Notes)

(1) In cases in which there exist Bills and Notes pertaining to my/our obligations, and your Bank makes deductions in accounts as set forth in Article 7 without exercising your Bank's rights on the Bills and Notes, your Bank need not simultaneously return to me/us any such Bills and Notes.

(2) In cases in which there exist Bills and Notes which your Bank returns to me/us as a result of deductions in accounts made by your Bank or me/us under the preceding two Articles, I/we shall appear at your Bank to receive such Bills and Notes without delay; provided, however, that if such Bills and Notes have not yet become due, your Bank may collect them without returning them to me/us.

(3) In cases in which your Bank makes deductions in accounts as set forth in Article 7 by exercising your Bank's rights on the Bills and Notes, your Bank need not present nor deliver any such Bills and Notes to me/us in the cases enumerated below; and as for my/our receiving such Bills and Notes, the provisions of the preceding Paragraph shall apply mutatis mutandis:

1. When your Bank does not know my/our whereabouts.
2. When I/we have designated your Bank as the place at which Bills and Notes are made payable.
3. When it is deemed difficult to dispatch the Bills and Notes.
4. When it is deemed that presentment or delivery of the Bills and Notes can not be made for unavoidable reasons as use for collection, etc.

(4) In cases in which any of my/our obligations which require immediate performance still exist after a deduction in accounts has been effected as provided for in the preceding two Articles, and there also exist obligors on the Bills and Notes besides me/us, your Bank may retain such Bills and Notes, and after collecting or disposing of them, your Bank may appropriate the proceeds to the payment of my/our obligations.

Article 9 (Designation of Appropriation)

In the event I/we made payments or your Bank made deductions in accounts as provided for in Article 7, and if in such cases the amount of such payments made by me/us or my/our deposits and any other credits with your Bank are insufficient to liquidate all of my/our obligations, your Bank may appropriate the amount of such payments or such deposits and other credits to satisfy my/our obligations in such order and in such manner as your Bank deems proper and I/we shall raise no objection to such appropriation.

Article 9-2   (Ditto)
   (1)   In the event I/we effect a setoff in accordance with Article 7-2, and if in such case my/our deposits and any other credits with your Bank are insufficient to liquidate all of my/our obligations, I/we may appropriate such deposits and other credits to satisfy my/our obligations in such order and in such manner as I/we designate.
   (2)   In the event I/we fail to designate the order and manner of appropriation under the preceding Paragraph, your Bank may appropriate my/our deposits and other credits with your Bank to satisfy my/our obligations in such order and in such manner as your Bank deems proper and I/we shall raise no objection to such appropriation.
   (3)   In the event my/our designation under Paragraph (1) is likely to interfere with the preservation of your Bank's rights, your Bank may, upon lodging an objection thereto without delay, appropriate my/our deposits and other credits with your Bank to satisfy my/our obligations in such order and in such manner as your Bank designates taking into consideration whether or not the obligations are secured or guaranteed and if secured or guaranteed, the extent of coverage of such security or guarantee, the degree of difficulty of disposition of such security, their due dates, prospects for settlement of discounted Bills and Notes, etc.
   (4)   In case of appropriation by your Bank under the preceding two Paragraphs, your Bank may designate the order and manner of appropriation on the assumption that my/our obligations which are in fact not due have become due or that I/we have assumed the repurchasing obligations with regard to the Bills and Notes which your Bank has discounted and which have not yet become due or that I/we have assumed in advance the obligations to compensate your Bank with regard to the acceptances and guarantees.

Article 10   (Assumption of Risks, Hold Harmless Clause, etc.)
   (1)   In cases in which Bills and Notes which I/we have drawn, endorsed, accepted, accepted by intervention or guaranteed, or instruments which I have furnished to your Bank are lost, destroyed, damaged or delayed in arrival due to unavoidable circumstances such as incidents, calamities, accidents during transit, etc., I/we shall pay my/our obligations as recorded on your Bank's books, vouchers, etc.; and further, upon your Bank's demand, I/we shall forthwith furnish your Bank with substitute Bills and Notes or instruments. I/we shall make no claim whatsoever against your Bank with regard to losses and damages arising in such cases.
   (2)   In cases in which security which I/we have furnished to your Bank is lost or damaged due to unavoidable circumstances as set forth in the preceding Paragraph, I/we shall make no claim whatsoever against your Bank.
   (3)   Even if your Bank's rights on Bills and Notes are ineffective due to lack of legal requirements in the Bills and Notes, or due to invalidating entries thereon, or if your Bank's rights on the Bills and Notes lapse due to inadequacy in the procedures for preservation of your Bank's rights, I/we shall be liable for the face value of such Bills and Notes.
   (4)   In transactions in which your Bank has deemed my/our seal impression or signature genuine after checking with reasonable care the seal impression or signature on Bills and Notes or instruments against my/our seal impression or specimen signature filed with your Bank, I/we shall bear any losses and damages arising from forgery, alteration, wrongful use of Bills and Notes, instruments or seals or signatures, and shall be liable in accordance with the terms of any such Bills and Notes or instruments.

(5)   I/we shall bear the expenses incurred in exercising or preserving your Bank's rights against me/us, or in collecting or disposing of any security; and I/we shall also bear any expenses required in the event I/we request your Bank to co-operate with me/us for the preservation of my/our rights.

Article 11   (Changes in Matters Filed)

(1)   In cases of a change in the matters filed with your Bank such as my/our seal or signature, name, trade name, representative, address, etc., I/we shall forthwith notify your Bank thereof in writing.

(2)   In case any notice given by your Bank or any documents, etc. dispatched by your Bank are delayed or fail to reach me/us because of my/our failure to notify your Bank in accordance with the preceding Paragraph, the notice or documents, etc. shall be deemed to have arrived at the time they normally should have arrived.

Article 12   (Report and Investigation)

(1)   Upon your Bank's demand, I/we shall forthwith submit to your Bank reports pertaining to my/our assets and liabilities, management or the state of business; and I/we shall also furnish assistance necessary for the investigation thereof.

(2)   In cases in which material change has occurred or is likely to occur pertaining to my/our assets and liabilities, management or the state of business, I/we shall forthwith submit to your Bank reports thereof even in the absence of your Bank's demand.

Article 13   (Applicable Offices)

I/we agree that all of the terms and conditions of this Agreement shall apply equally to all of my/our transactions with your Bank's head office and branch offices.

Article 14   (Jurisdiction by Agreement)

In the event the institution of a lawsuit in connection with a transaction covered by this Agreement becomes necessary, I/we shall agree that the Court having the jurisdiction in the locale in which the head office or _____ _____ branch office of your Bank is situated shall be the competent Court.

In regard to any and all obligations the Principal may owe your Bank as a result of transactions provided for in Article 1, the Guarantor shall be jointly and severally liable with the Principal for the performance of all such obligations, and the Guarantor hereby agrees to abide by the terms and conditions of this Agreement with regard to the performance of any such obligations.

The Guarantor shall not set off any obligations which the Principal may owe your Bank under this Agreement against any of the Principal's deposits and/or any other credits with your Bank.

Even if your Bank changes or releases the security or other guarantees at your Bank's convenience, the Guarantor shall not claim exemption from the obligations.

If and when the Guarantor performs any obligations of guarantee, the Guarantor shall not exercise any rights obtained from your Bank by subrogation without the prior approval of your Bank as long as transactions between the Principal and your Bank continue. Upon your Bank's demand, the Guarantor shall assign such rights and priority to your Bank without compensation.

Dated this _____ day of _____ Nineteen Hundred and _____

The Principal

Signature:

| Revenue | Full Name: | L.S. |
| Stamp | Address: |

The Guarantor

Signature: L.S.

Full Name:

Address:

(All questions that may arise within or without courts of law in regard to the meaning of the words, provisions and stipulations of this Agreement shall be decided in accordance with the Japanese text.)

New financial products in Japan

Masabumi Yamane
General Manager
Legal Department
The Bank of Tokyo, Ltd

1. The liberalization and internationalization of the Japanese monetary system

The last decade has seen a rapid, but steady, liberalization and internationalization of the Japanese monetary system. This has developed in a unique way in Japan, as compared with other countries.

The liberalization and internationalization of the Japanese monetary system has comprised a two-tiered policy; first in the internationalization of the yen, secondly in the introduction of foreign monetary systems and foreign financial products into the Japanese money markets.

This liberalization has developed through the lifting of various cumbersome regulatory restrictions hitherto imposed on financial transactions.

Since May 1984, the month in which the Ministry of Finance (MOF) published its report entitled 'The Present Situation and Future Direction in Respect of the Internationalization of the Monetary System', officially announcing its new, forward-looking fiscal policy, the liberalization and internationalization of the Japanese monetary system and money markets have rapidly developed. That development further accelerated with the publication of MOF's report entitled 'Japanese-American Yen-Dollar Committee Report', which called for the liberalization of international currency transactions involving the Japanese yen.[1]

The liberalization and internationalization of the Japanese monetary system and money markets has both allowed for and been accelerated by the

---

[1] For the latest account of liberalization of financial markets in Japan, see B. W. Semkow, 'The Deregulation of Japan's Financial Markets', *International Financial Law Review* (August 1987) p 34ff. Also Semkow, 'Japanese Banking Law: Current Deregulation and Liberalization of Domestic and External Financial Transactions', *Law and Policy in International Business* (vol 17, 1985), pp 137–155. S. Bronte, 'The Japanese Financial System in 1990', in ABA Practical Law Institute ed, *Legal Aspects of Doing Business with Japan* (New York, 1985) pp 15–30.

introduction of certain foreign financial products into the Japanese monetary system, perhaps the most important event in the last twenty years of Japanese fiscal history. Those products include:

(1) CD's (an abbreviation for Negotiable Time Certificate of Deposit, *jyoutosei teiki yokin shousho*), (2) MMC's (Money Market Certificate, *shijyou kinri rendougata yokin*), (3) BA's (Bankers' Acceptance, *ginkou hikiuke tegata*), (4) Mortgage Debentures (*teitou shoken*) or Mortgage Certificate (*teitou shousho*), and (5) CP's (Commercial Paper), each of which have been recently introduced into (or further developed within) the Japanese monetary system.[2]

Features of these will be outlined below.

2. CD's

On 30 March 1979 the Ministry of Finance announced that it would henceforth allow financial institutions to enter into negotiable certificates of deposit transactions. This Notification (Director of the Banking Bureau, MOF, hereafter *kuragin* No 650), entitled 'As to the Transactions of Negotiable Certificates of Deposit', as amended by the Notification of 31 March 1980 (*kuragin* No 750), the Notification of 27 January 1983 (*kuragin* No 150) and the Notification of 11 March 1988 (*kuragin* No 400), established the following as the material characteristics of the Japanese CD product:

(1) Name: The product shall be called 'Negotiable Certificate of Deposit'.

(2) Transferability: Transferable in accordance with regulations governing assignment of claims generally.

(3) Unit of issuance: Each certificate of deposit shall be in an amount not less than 100 million Japanese yen (approx 800,000 dollars, this amount has been gradually reduced from 500 million Japanese yen. MOF has an intention to reduce this amount to 50 million Japanese yen as from April 1988.)

(4) Maturity: Each certificate of deposit shall have a maturity not less than two weeks or more than two years from the date of issue. (The range of maturities represents a broadening from the original maturities of not less than three months and not more than six months from the date of issue.) The maturity of each certificate of deposit is determined by the depositor at issuance, and after the maturity interest on the certificate of deposit shall not be paid. (In respect of certificates of deposit the term of which is two years, interest on the certificate of deposit shall be payable on the anniversary date of the issuance thereof; otherwise, all accrued interest in respect of any outstanding certificate of deposit shall be due and payable on the maturity date of such certificate.)

---

[2] See also A. Viner, *Inside Japan's Financial Markets* (London, 1987) pp 194–203.

(5) Method of issuance: Each certificate of deposit shall be issued upon the execution of an agreement between the depositor and the depository bank.

(6) Limitation of amount of issuance: (a) The aggregate balance of outstanding certificates of deposit issued by any financial institution (except Japanese branches of foreign banks) is not permitted to exceed 75% of such institution's owned capital. (MOF removed this restriction recently.) (b) The aggregate outstanding balance of certificates of deposit issued by any Japanese branch or branches of a foreign bank is not permitted to exceed the higher of (i) 30% of the aggregate amount expressed in Japanese yen of loan accounts and marketable securities accounts of such branch or branches, or, (ii) 5 billion Japanese yen. (MOF removed this restriction recently.)

(7) Interest rate: Pursuant to Notification No 4 of the Ministry of Finance of 1948, as amended, interest rates for Negotiable Certificates of Deposit are subject only to general usury laws.

(8) Prior cancellation and redemption by purchase: The depositor shall not be entitled to cancel the certificate of deposit prior to its maturity and the depository bank shall not purchase its issued certificate of deposits for redemption.

(9) Definitions of terms and the details of procedures in respect of certificates of deposit are regulated by other provisions of the Notification (*kuragin* No 650) not mentioned herein and by several other Notifications, regulations and provisions issued by the National Association of Bankers.

3. MMC's

On the assumption that the introduction of a system in which certificate of deposit rates are free to reflect prevailing money rate levels in the money market would contribute much to the promotion of liberalization of the Japanese monetary system, the Ministry of Finance announced the inauguration of the money market certificate product by issuing a Notification (*kuragin* No 250) dated 14 February 1985 entitled 'As to Dealings in Money Market Certificates', the material contents of which are as follows:

(1) Name: Money Market Certificate.

(2) Term: Between one and six months. The maturity of each certificate shall be determined at the time of deposit by the depositor and interest on the certificate shall not be paid after the maturity thereof.

(3) Amount of deposit: The amount of each certificate should be at least 10 million Japanese yen. This minimum amount requirement has been reduced recently.

(4) Interest rate: The rate of interest applicable to each certificate shall be

determined independently by the relevant financial institution taking into account the maturity of each certificate, provided that any such interest rate shall not exceed the maximum rate determined in accordance with the Notification No 14 of the MOF of 9 February 1980 entitled 'In re: Maximum Interest Rate of Financial Institutions Applicable to Money Market Certificates'.

(5) Limitation on amount of deposit: (a) The aggregate balance of outstanding certificates issued by any financial institution (except Japanese branches of foreign banks) is not permitted to exceed 75% of such institution's owned capital. (b) The aggregate outstanding balance of certificates issued by any Japanese branch or branches of a foreign bank is not permitted to exceed the higher of (i) 30% of the aggregate amount expressed in Japanese yen of loan accounts and marketable securities accounts of such branch or branches, or, (ii) 5 billion Japanese yen. (c) If, in respect of any financial institution, foreign or domestic, the aggregate outstanding balance of negotiable certificate of deposit is at any time less than the amount permitted by this Notification, 25% of the difference between the amount permitted by this Notification and the aggregate amount then outstanding may be added to the amount permitted by this Notification for purposes of issuing certificates subsequent to such time. (MOF removed these restrictions recently.)

(6) Method of deposit: Each financial institution may determine the method of deposit for each certificate in consultation with the depositor, or a standardized form for the transaction may be adopted.

(7) Cancellation: Within one month from the date of issue, the depositor shall, in principle, not be entitled to cancel a certificate. If any certificate shall nonetheless be cancelled because of unforeseen circumstances, no interest shall be payable in respect of such certificate, although the principal amount of the certificate shall be recoverable upon cancellation. If any certificate is cancelled on or after the date one month from the date of issue and prior to the maturity date thereof, the rate of interest prevailing on such cancellation date applicable to a savings account shall apply to such certificate. Certificates may not be cancelled in part or divided.

(8) Prohibition of assignment or pledge: A depository bank shall obtain a covenant from a depositor that any certificate shall not be assigned or pledged. This treatment is different from that of Negotiable Certificates of Deposit.

(9) Definitions and procedures relating to certificates of deposit are established by other provisions of the Notification (*kuragin* No 250) not discussed herein and by several other Notifications, regulations and provisions issued by the National Association of Bankers.

4. BA's

Since 1975, there has been much debate regarding whether to open a Bankers' Acceptance Market in Japan. Such a market would enable certain financial institutions engaged in Japanese yen denominated trade financing to obtain funds necessary to settle such trade financings. The increased risk arising as a result of the recent exchange rate volatility and the high US dollar interest rate has fueled the debate and accelerated the opening of the Bankers' Acceptance Market in Japan.

By a Notification (*kuragin* No 667) dated 1 April 1985, MOF permitted the opening of a Bankers' Acceptance Market in Japan with effect from 1 June 1985.

The material characteristics of the Notification (*kuragin* No 667) are as follows:

(1) Yen Denominated Eligible Bills of Exchange:

The five bills of exchange described below may each be duly accepted by an authorized foreign exchange bank in connection with any foreign trade transaction, provided such acceptance shall have occurred (i) in respect of bills of exchange drawn by a Japanese exporter, within 30 days of the date of issuance of such bills, or (ii) in respect of bills of exchange other than the represented bills of exchange referred to in (e) below and bills of exchange drawn by Japanese exporters, within 45 days of the date of issuance, provided that such bills of exchange must mature within six months of the date of issue plus a certain number of days for mailing:

(a) Yen Denominated Trade Bills of Exchange with Letter of Credit (*shinyoujyou tsuki endate boueki tegata*): Yen denominated trade bills drawn on an authorized foreign exchange bank as payee under a letter of credit.

(b) Accommodation Bills of Exchange (Accommodation *tegata*): Accommodation bills of exchange under this Notification are Japanese yen Denominated Bills of Exchange (other than the bills of exchange referred to in (a) above) that are drawn on an authorized foreign exchange bank located in Japan for the settlement of foreign trade transactions and are (i) drawn by a domestic exporter as payee and purchased by an authorized foreign exchange bank in Japan, or (ii) drawn by an exporter located outside Japan and purchased by a principal office or branch office of an authorized foreign exchange bank also located outside Japan.

(c) Import Settlement Relation Bills of Exchange (*yunyū kessai kanren tegata*, so called '*jiki hane tegata*'): Yen Denominated Bills of Exchange drawn by an importer (domestic or foreign), as payee, on an authorized foreign exchange bank located in Japan in connection with the Japanese yen denominated financing of an import transaction, payment terms of which are at sight, etc.

(d) Refinance Bills of Exchange (Refinance *tegata*): Yen Denominated Bills of Exchange drawn by foreign banks granting yen denominated trade finance advances pursuant to a Yen Denominated Bill of Exchange (other than a bill of exchange referred to in (a) above) drawn by an exporter, as payee, on an authorized foreign exchange bank (except a branch of such foreign bank located in Japan) for the settlement of foreign trade transactions.

(e) Represented Bills of Exchange (*hyoushi tegata*): Yen Denominated Bills of Exchange drawn by an authorized foreign exchange bank located in Japan on itself as security for the bills of exchange referred to in (a) through to (d) inclusive. Such bills of exchange are to be deposited with The Bank of Japan.

(2) Minimum Denomination of Yen Denominated Bankers' Acceptance Bills of Exchange Available for Sale to the Public: Authorized foreign exchange banks are permitted to sell Yen Denominated Bankers' Acceptance Bills of Exchange to the public, provided that each such bill of exchange shall have a face amount of at least 100 million Japanese yen (approx 800,000 dollars).

(3) Any authorized foreign exchange bank located in Japan that has accepted yen denominated bankers' acceptance bills of exchange shall be entitled to sell such bills of exchange only for its own account and shall not return any bills of exchange so accepted to the drawer directly.

(4) Definitions and procedures relating to yen denominated bankers' acceptance bills of exchange are established by other provisions of the Notification (*kuragin* No 667) not discussed herein and by several other circulars of MOF and regulations and provisions issued by the National Association of Bankers.

5. Mortgage debenture

Banks are permitted to participate in the mortgage instrument business through their related companies pursuant to the Notification (*kuragin* No 1968 of 3 July 1975) entitled 'The Relationship Between Financial Institutions and Their Related Companies'. City banks (other than The Bank of Tokyo Ltd) are actively engaged in the mortgage instrument business through their subsidiaries.

The mortgage instrument business is subject to the Law on Mortgage Debentures (Law No 15, 1931) (*teitou shouken hou*).

Pursuant to Article 1 of the Law on Mortgage Debentures, one who has been granted a mortgage on land, building structure, or 'superficies' is entitled to apply to the land registry office for the issuance of a mortgage debenture.[3]

---

[3] 'Mortgage' is one of the real securities over immovables provided by the Civil Code. In case of default, a mortgagee is entitled to receive the proceeds of sale of the property in preference to other creditors, but he does not have the title to the property. In this sense, Japanese '*teitou ken*' is closer to a hypothec. For real security rights, H. Tanikawa, et al, eds, *Credit and Security in Japan* (St. Lucia, NY, 1973) pp 53–137.

The mortgage instrument business is transacted as follows:

(i) A debtor (ie, a borrower) requests a creditor (who will apply to the land registry office for the issuance of a mortgage debenture) to grant a loan facility, which facility shall be secured by the mortgage.

(ii) The creditor makes the loan to a debtor. (Items (ii) through (vii), inclusive, should occur substantially simultaneously.)

(iii) The creditor applies to the competent land registry office for a mortgage debenture by submitting an application for the issuance of a mortgage debenture accompanied by the requisite documentation.

(iv) The officer of the land registry office examines the submitted documents and checks whether or not such documentation is complete.

(v) The land registry office, upon its confirmation that such documents are complete, issues a mortgage debenture and delivers the same to the creditor.

(vi) The creditor delivers the mortgage debenture to a bank, which will act as custodian for the creditor.

(vii) The bank issues a certificate of deposit of mortgage debenture and delivers the same to the creditor.

(viii) An investor who intends to make an investment in the mortgage debenture pays money in respect of such mortgage debenture to the creditor.

(ix) A creditor may sell his interest in a mortgage debenture (or any portion thereof) to an investor or investors, but actual delivery of the mortgage debenture to any such investor shall not occur. (The bank will continue to hold the mortgage debenture as mentioned in (vii) above.) The rationale for this arrangement is that (i) if an investor lost his mortgage debenture, it would be difficult to enforce such investor's rights as holder since mortgage debentures are freely transferable negotiable instruments, (ii) it is not practical to record title to the mortgage debenture with the land registry office since a mortgage debenture may be divided into a great many pieces, (iii) loans secured by mortgages generally have maturities of 20 years or more, while an investor's interest in the mortgage debenture arising out of such a loan is not more than five years, and (iv) debtors typically wish to avoid disclosing their names to unspecified investors (the name of the debtor and the security condition of the loan are stipulated on the face of the mortgage debenture).

In lieu of delivery of a mortgage debenture, the creditor delivers to the investor its mortgage certificate (*teitou shousho*).

(x) The debtor pays interest on the loan to the creditor.

(xi) The creditor pays interest in respect of the mortgage certificate to the investor.

(xii) The debtor repays the principal amount of the loan to the creditor.

(xiii) The creditor repays the principal amount in respect of the mortgage certificate to the investor.

In practice, mortgage instrument business differs from that as provided by the Law on Mortgage Debentures since over a half of a century has passed from the time that the Law was enacted. In particular, as mentioned above, a creditor delivers only a mortgage certificate to an investor purchasing an interest in a mortgage debenture, not the mortgage debenture itself. A mortgage certificate is merely evidence that a creditor has received the money for a mortgage debenture from an investor and does not independently assure the investor that a mortgage debenture has been duly issued by a land registry office. A mortgage certificate states only the purchase price of the certificate, the rate of interest, the maturity date of the certificate, the registration number of the underlying mortgage debenture and the land registry office. The mortgage certificate does not state the name and address of the debtor, the maturity of debt secured by the mortgage debenture and the mortgaged property (all of which are stated in the mortgage debenture). In the past, individual investors have been damaged because a mortgage debenture they purchased turned out not to be secured by an actual mortgage on the purportedly mortgaged property.

For the protection of individual investors, The Law on the Regulations of the Mortgage Instrument Business (Law No 114, 1987, *teitou shouken gyou no kisei tou ni kansuru houritsu*) has been enacted.

6. CP's

On 20 November 1987, with MOF's publication of a Notification (*kuragin* No 2825 of 2 November 1987) entitled 'As to the treatment of Commercial Paper to be Issued in Japan', Japan achieved one of the principal goals of the internationalization of the Japanese yen. The establishment of a commercial paper market in Japan. Such a market, it had been argued, would both greatly enhance the services provided by, and the expansion of, the Japanese short-term financial markets.

This Notification relates only to commercial paper issued in Japan; domestic CP in short (*kokunai* Commercial Paper) by financial institutions other than securities companies and call brokers (*tanshi gyousha*).

Commercial paper issued in Japan and managed by securities companies is subject to the Notification (*kurashou* No 1830 of 2 November 1987) entitled 'On the Treatment by Security Companies of Commercial Paper to be Issued in Japan', the content of which is nearly identical to that of Notification No 2825.

Notification No 2825 established the following as the material characteristics of the various Japanese commercial paper products:

(i) Domestic CP under this Notification means non-secured, short-term 'promissory notes' (*yakusoku tegata*) issued by 'Top ranked enterprises' (*yūryou kigyo*) in Japan to 'institutional investors' (*kikan toushika*). Domestic CP's must comply with the following three conditions:
(a) the term of each Domestic CP note shall be between one month and six months,

(b) interest on a Domestic CP note shall be paid on a discounted basis, and

(c) the face amount of each Domestic CP note shall be not less than 100 million Japanese yen (approx 800,000 dollars).

(ii) Financial institutions other than securities companies may engage in the sale and purchase of Domestic CP's, may act as intermediaries in sale and purchase transactions, may act as agent to either of the parties in a Domestic CP transaction and may conduct other business in respect of Domestic CP's. Call brokers may engage only in sale and purchase transactions and only at the time such transactions are negotiated.

(iii) Financial institutions shall act as dealers of Domestic CP's and shall examine the financial condition of the issuing company and the availability of back up lines of credit or bank guarantees with a view towards protection of the interests of potential investors. Top ranked enterprises that have been declared eligible to issue unsecured bonds and the eleven enterprises such as electric power companies that have been authorized to issue bonds secured by 'general security' (*ippan tanpo tsuki shasai*) are eligible to issue Domestic CP's supported by a back up line of credit or a bank guarantee. Certain authorized enterprises may not be required to provide such forms of credit support for their Domestic CP's.

(iv) Domestic CP's shall be issued and distributed in the market as 'dealer paper'. CP's shall be sold through a sales agent and shall not be sold directly by the issuing company to investors.

(v) At the time of issuance, financial institutions acting as dealers for such issue shall each prepare statements describing in detail the corporation making such issue.

(vi) Domestic CP's may not be sold to individual investors.

(vii) Financial institutions shall prepare records in respect of transactions involving Domestic CP's and shall keep such records at their offices.

(viii) Definitions and procedures relating to Domestic CP's are established by other provisions of the Notification No 2825 not discussed herein and by several other circulars of the MOF and regulations and provisions issued by the National Association of Bankers (including model forms of various documents to be executed in connection with Domestic CP transactions).

Typical Domestic CP issuances proceed as follows:

(i) A company ('CP issuer') decides to issue Domestic CP's and drafts an 'issuing plan'.

Each 'issuing plan' shall contain (a) a statement of the aggregate amount of Domestic CP's to be issued, (b) an appointment of a Domestic CP dealer (which shall be a bank or a security company), (c) an appointment of a back-up line bank or a guarantee bank, (d) an appointment of a Domestic CP paying agent bank, and (e) an appointment of a Domestic CP issuing agent (which shall also be a bank or a securities company), if the CP Issuer wishes to appoint such agent.

(ii) The CP Issuer shall execute the following documents, among others:
  (a) the Domestic CP Dealer Agreement,
  (b) the Domestic CP Back-Up Line Agreement (or Guarantee Agreement),
  (c) the Domestic CP Paying Agency Agreement, and
  (d) the Domestic CP Issuing Agency Agreement (if the CP Issuer appoints an issuing agent for the issue).

(iii) The CP Issuer shall open a 'Current Account Only For The Settlement Of Domestic CP' with the Domestic CP Paying Agent, from which the payment of Domestic CP's shall be made.

(iv) The CP Issuer, or a Domestic CP dealer relying on information provided by the CP Issuer, shall prepare a report entitled 'Statement Regarding the CP Issuer etc' for delivery to or inspection by potential investors. Such statement shall set forth a summary description of the CP Issuer and the terms of the Domestic CP's to be issued.

(v) Where an issuing agent is appointed, the CP Issuer shall issue blank promissory notes stating only face values and deliver the same to the issuing agent prior to the issuance of the Domestic CP's.

(vi) The Domestic CP dealer shall confirm that (a) the CP Issuer is eligible to issue Domestic CP's, and (b) the existence of a back-up line provided by a back-up line bank or the existence of a guarantee of the CP by a guarantee bank.

(vii) The CP Issuer and the Domestic CP dealer shall agree, at least two business days prior to the issue date of the Domestic CP's on the terms of the Domestic CP pursuant to which the Domestic CP dealer will purchase the relevant CP's on the issue date.

(viii) The CP Issuer delivers to the back-up line bank an 'issuing statement' (*hakkou meisaisho*) containing the amount and maturity of the CP issue once such terms have been determined.

(ix) The CP Issuer shall deliver the CP notes together with a 'delivery statement' (*koufu meisaisho*) prior to 11:00 am on the date of issue thereof to the place designated by the Domestic CP dealer.

(x) The Domestic CP dealer shall deliver a receipt for the CP notes to the CP Issuer upon its confirmation of the terms contained in the delivery statement. Immediately thereafter, the Domestic CP dealer shall pay the purchase price discounted at the agreed rate to the bank account of the CP Issuer designated in such delivery statement.

(xi) The domestic CP dealer shall sell the Domestic CP's purchased by it to investors. Sometimes, at the request of such investor, Domestic CP's purchased by the investor have to be deposited with a bank to be held in custody for the investor.

(xii) At the direction of the CP Issuer contained in the 'application for issue' (*hakkou iraisho*), the issuing agent shall inscribe the Domestic CP notes with the date of issue and the maturity date and, prior to 11:00 am on the issue date, shall deliver a completed Domestic CP (stamped with the necessary revenue stamp) to the Domestic CP dealer together with a delivery statement.

In addition to Domestic CP transactions, the Ministry of Finance has subsequently permitted Non-resident Euro-Yen CP transactions and Non-resident Domestic CP (so called '*samurai* CP' or *hikyojūsha hakkou kokunai* CP) transactions, subject to certain terms and conditions.

Loan securities and negotiable instruments

Hiroshi Kinoshita
Partner
Tokyo Aoyama Law Office

1. Guarantees and collateral (real) security

GUARANTEES

Needless to say, guarantees (suretyship) and collateral security are extremely important devices to protect creditor's interests. Banks, for example, do not, and perhaps should not, lend money to others without a proper guarantee or collateral security.

Banks frequently require a guarantor when extending a loan. Normally, the parent company, the affiliate, or the president of the borrowing company serves as the guarantor. When necessary, a bank may sometimes act as a guarantor in return for a certain guarantee fee. In a banking transaction (eg, a loan) the guarantee is almost always joint and several.

In theory, a guarantee may not offer better protection for creditors than collateral security because if the guarantor cannot perform his obligation under the guarantee, the creditor will end up with no protection. On the other hand, if necessary measures to prevail against third parties are taken, in other words if the security interest is duly perfected, collateral security is an ideal means for protection of the creditor's interest since the assets are always there at the ultimate disposal of the creditor.

Nevertheless, guarantees are frequently used in the business world, including bank transactions. The reason for this is that as long as the creditor is not apprehensive about any deterioration of the guarantor's financial position for the period of guarantee, the guarantee procedure is quite simple, as will be mentioned later. Furthermore, collectability is virtually always 100% since guarantors with good social standing always make their best effort to perform under their guarantee liability, even borrowing the necessary funds from another bank if necessary.[1]

---

[1] Provisions on personal security—suretyship can be found in Part Three (Law of Obligation) of the Civil Code (Arts 446–465).

Classification

There are two types of guarantee: (1) ordinary guarantee and (2) joint and several guarantee.

The major differences between the 'ordinary guarantee' and the 'joint and several guarantee' are as follows:

1. While the ordinary guarantor may assert that the obligee should first demand payment against the obligor or collect from the obligor first, the joint and several guarantor has no such right: so long as there exists an underlying obligation, a joint and several guarantor is subject at any time to a claim by the obligee. Accordingly, a joint and several guarantor may raise no objection to the obligee's demand for payment or enforcement against his property even before the obligee acts against the obligor.

2. If there are two ordinary guarantors, the guarantee liability will be shared by both guarantors, ie, each guarantor will be liable to the obligee up to 50% of the obligation duty. On the other hand in the case of joint and several guarantors, each such guarantor is fully liable to the obligee.

3. While a notice of demand to an ordinary guarantor does not interrupt the running of the statute of limitations, notice of demand to a joint and several guarantor does interrupt running of the statute of limitations in respect of the principal debt.

Guarantor's rights against obligor upon payment of debt

(1) SUBROGATION

The guarantor is entitled to exercise the rights, including rights in collateral security, which the obligee had against the obligor.

(2) REIMBURSEMENT

The principal obligor must reimburse the guarantor for any amount the guarantor has paid by reason of the guarantee.

Article 504 of the Civil Code provides that a guarantor who can be subrogated to the rights of the creditor may be exempt from the liability to the extent of the loss or reduction in value of the security caused by the intentional or negligent act of the creditor. To avoid application of Article 504, in practice, banks usually include in their standard form of agreement on bank transactions a provision to the effect that: 'In regard to any and all present or future obligations the Principal Debtor may owe your Bank, the Guarantor hereby agreeing to the terms and conditions of this Agreement shall be jointly and severally liable with the Principal debtor for the performance of all obligations, and *shall not object to your Bank's changing or releasing the security or other guarantees at your Bank's convenience.*'

Joint and several guarantors

As stated earlier, in commercial transactions, the obligee almost always requires that the guarantor be jointly and severally liable with the obligor. This joint and several guarantor is called *rentai hoshounin*, *rentai* literally means 'bound together' and *hoshounin* means 'guarantor(s)'.

The liability of the joint and several guarantor (*rentai hoshounin*) is almost the same as that of the principal obligor. The most outstanding feature of the *rentai hoshounin* is that he may raise no objection to the creditor even if the creditor demands payment from him before demanding payment from the obligor. The *rentai hoshounin*'s liability will cease, however, if the principal obligor's liability turns out to be invalid, cancelled or otherwise discharged. The independence of the *rentai hoshounin*'s liability from that of the principal obligor is, therefore, limited to that extent.

Formalities

As to formalities, the guarantor must sign or place his seal on the guarantee agreement (in theory, however, even a verbal guarantee is valid). Beyond that, unlike in some other jurisdictions, no special formalities, eg, registration, are required to make a guarantee effective.

In theory, a guarantee may take the form of a unilateral pledge to the creditor or a guarantee agreement concluded between the guarantor and obligee. In practice, however, most guarantee agreements take the form of a three-party contract.

In the past, a guarantee agreement between an exchange resident and an exchange non-resident was subject to the governmental approval under the Foreign Exchange Control Law. Such restrictions, however, were removed ten years ago owing to the significant liberalisation of the law, and therefore no notification to the government is currently required for a transnational guarantee.

Regardless of whether he is an ordinary guarantor or a *rentai hoshounin*, a guarantor is in principle given the right of subrogation and reimbursement. Such basic rights of the guarantor, however, are often subject to limitations by way of special agreements with banks.

Practice note

In banking circles, a letter of comfort is often issued by a parent company with respect to the debts owned by its subsidiary. A letter of comfort is used, of course, mainly because the parent company does not want to increase its liability by way of a formal guarantee but rather prefers to substitute a mere moral obligation for the liability. While the contents of such a letter of comfort vary, most letters of comfort provide 'we will do our best so as to enable our subsidiary to repay the loan without delay, and if your bank deems it necessary we will negotiate with your bank in good faith regarding the guarantee with respect thereto.' It is generally believed that such a letter of comfort does not legally bind the issuer as a guarantor. However, at least domestically, such a letter will put the recipient thereof in a strong position, especially where the issuer thereof is a reputable company.

COLLATERAL (REAL) SECURITY

There are various kinds of collateral security. Several of the more important types of securities that are commonly used in commercial transactions in Japan will be discussed below.[2]

Immovable assets (real property)

Real property is widely used as collateral since its value is generally stable and, particularly with respect to land, the value rarely decreases. However, since real property is not readily marketable, foreclosure by banks is generally a last resort.

Real security attaches to specific property of the obligor and/or that of a third person. Depending on the types of property, real security may be classified as follows:

(1) Mortgage (hypothec)
(2) Base-mortgage (securing possible future obligations)
(3) Real property pledge
(4) Preliminary registration security
(5) Assignment as security.

Real property is widely used as the subject of collateral security to secure debts, especially relatively long-term loans. However, because perfection of a collateral security interest in real property usually requires cumbersome procedures and considerable expense in the form of a registration tax, banks and other creditors tend to eschew this security device, if another simpler device with the same degree of security is available.

The most frequently used security device involving real property is probably the mortgage (hypothec or *teitou*). This security device does not require the mortgagor to transfer title or possession of the mortgaged property to the mortgagee until and unless the mortgagor defaults. Thus, the Japanese mortgage is juristically similar to hypothec in the Continental legal system. That is to say, it transfers only a special security interest to the mortgagee. The mortgage right is created when the mortgagor and the mortgagee enter into a mortgage agreement. For the mortgagee to prevail against a third party, such as another creditor, a third party purchaser, lessee successor or receiver, however, the mortgagee must have registered the mortgage before the third party's rights have been perfected.[3]

---

[2] For real security rights, see H. Tanikawa, et al, eds, *Credit and Security in Japan* (St. Lucia, NY, 1973). This book was published before the enactment of the Law on Security by Preliminary Registration in 1978.
[3] Arts 369–398, Civil Code.

Similar to mortgage is the base mortgage (*ne-teitou*). *Ne* literally means 'root', but it is used to mean that one basic mortgage covers many future unspecified debts between the bank and its customer up to a certain maximum amount and time.[4]

Pledge over immovables (*fudosan-shichi*) is another form of security. *Fudosan* means 'real (immovable) property' and *shichi* means 'pledge'. This device, known as *antichresis* in the civil law, requires the pledgor to transfer possession (though not the title) to the pledgee. Since banks are not generally interested in taking possession of real property, resort to this device is not common.[5]

Another device, codified ten years ago, is what is known as the 'provisional registration security' (*kari-touki-tampo*: Law No 78, 1978). *Kari* means 'preliminary' or 'provisional'; *touki* means 'registration' and *tampo* means 'security'. The basic mechanism is that the obligor enters into an agreement to substitute title to real property for the monetary debt conditional upon default and the obligee registers the contingent right acquired under that substitution agreement under special registration system called *kari-touki* or 'provisional registration'.

Finally, another means of obtaining a security interest in real property without transferring possession of the property is an 'assignment as security' or *jouto tampo* (*jouto* means 'assignment'). This practice has not been codified in any statute, but is widely recognised as a valid form of security.

In an assignment as security, the obligor assigns his property to the obligee, thus passing the title to the obligee. The obligor and obligee agree, however, that this assignment is solely for the purpose of security and that, once the debt is fully repaid, the obligee must return title in the property to the obligor. Such a security interest must also be registered in order for it to prevail against a third person. The registration will be cancelled when the debt is repaid in full.

Movable assets (personal property)

Some non-bank creditors take movable assets such as machines or product inventory as collateral by way of pledge or assignment as security, although such assets are less satisfactory than those mentioned earlier from the standpoint of protecting the creditor's interests because of their lesser marketability. Banking practice does not normally accept these assets as collateral.

For certain movable assets, such as automobiles, aircraft or ships, for which registration systems exist, a security interest may be perfected by registration. Consequently, a pledgee or assignee of such an asset may acquire a security interest and assert it against any third party without taking possession of the asset. This device was created by merchants a long time ago and was finally codified some fifteen years ago.

[4] Arts 398-2 to 398-22, Civil Code.
[5] Arts 356–361, Civil Code.
[6] Tanikawa et al, supra, pp 120–137.

Negotiable instruments

The collateral security most frequently taken by banks is probably in shares and bonds or debentures. Because negotiable instruments are highly liquid and readily marketable, banks generally welcome them as collateral. There are two mechanisms for creating a security interest in negotiable instruments: (1) assignment as security and (2) pledge. Of the two, banks tend to prefer the 'assignment as security' approach because it puts the bank in a better position with regard to conflicting claims by the tax authorities to the same asset.

It is generally necessary to acquire possession of the assets for the assignee or pledgee to prevail against a third party creditor, however, in the case of assignment as security, the assignor may retain possession by substituting notice of the assignment. To prevail against a third party, while there must be delivery in the cases of both bearer and order papers, the latter must in addition be endorsed for security purposes.

In some rare cases, banks may accept accounts receivable or loan obligation rights as collateral. It is necessary for the bank to give notice to the third party obligor or to obtain consent from the third party obligor. Furthermore such notice or consent must be dated and notarised if the bank is to prevail against a third party creditor.

Rights of an obligee

Bank deposits, accounts receivable and insurance claims are often taken by banks as security, under a (1) pledge, (2) assignment as security, (3) acceptance of payment in lieu of the obligee (*dairi-bensai juryou*) or (4) designation of a transfer account (*furikomi shitei*).

One final special device creates a comprehensive security interest in certain assets as a whole, similar to the English floating charge. This is the *kigyou tampo. Kigyou* means 'enterprise'. This security interest attaches not to specific assets of the enterprise but rather to all of its assets: which include land, factory buildings, office buildings, machinery, inventory, accounts receivable, intellectual property rights. This security interest attaches and is perfected only if duly registered. This device, however, is not used frequently, since the only debt that can be secured in this way is either (1) debts arising out of bond issues and (2) loans from the Japan Development Bank. Furthermore, to be permitted to utilise this device, the mortgagor company must satisfy certain financial requirements, eg, it must be capitalised at no less than 30 billion yen, have net assets of at least 45 billion yen, and so forth. There are numerous limitations on its effectiveness, such as, for example, the *kigyou tampo* is always subordinated to any other perfected security interest regardless of the time of perfection.

The following is a sample guarantee agreement adopted by most banks in Japan:

GUARANTY AGREEMENT

To:

Guarantor   Name:

Address:

Debtor   Name:

Address:

The Guarantor, pursuant to transactions prescribed in Article 1 of the Bank Transaction Agreement separately provided by the Debtor, bears jointly with the Debtor guaranteed obligations with respect to all obligations borne now and in the future with respect to your Bank, and, in the performance thereof, will obey the following provisions, as well as the provisions of the aforementioned Bank Transaction Agreement.

Article 1:
The maximum amount of the guaranteed obligations shall be _____ yen and shall include all obligations which arise from transactions up until _____ 19__, regardless of whether it is before or after the day this Guaranty Agreement is provided. However, if there is no notice from your Bank the above time limit shall be extended for one year.

Article 2:
The Guarantor will not offset by means of the Debtor's deposits or other claims against your Bank.

Article 3:
The Guarantor will claim no discharge even if your Bank for its own convenience alters or cancels the security or other guaranty.

Article 4:
In the event the Guarantor performs the guaranteed obligations, rights acquired from your Bank by subrogation will not be exercised during the continuance of transactions between the Debtor and your Bank without your Bank's consent. Upon demand by your Bank, such rights or ranking will be assigned to your Bank without compensation.

Article 5:
(1) If the Guarantor otherwise makes a guaranty with respect to transactions between the Debtor and your Bank, such guaranty shall be unaltered by this guaranty agreement, and if any other guaranty is made which has a maximum-amount provision, then such maximum amount of the guaranty shall be added to the amount of this guaranty.
(2) The preceding paragraph may be applied correspondingly if in the future the Guarantor makes a guaranty with respect to your Bank.

2. Negotiable instruments

BILLS, NOTES AND CHEQUES

In domestic transactions, the importance of promissory notes as opposed to bills of exchange is overwhelming, perhaps in the order of 99 against 1.

Use in relation with bank loans (*tegata-kashitsuke*)

A bank usually requires a documentary loan agreement and real property security for a long-term loan. On the other hand, for shorter term loans, three to six months, a bank will normally require instead of a loan agreement a promissory note in the amount of the loan. Of course, banks also require the execution of a Standard Agreement on Bank Transactions as well. The reasons for the use of this method are:

(1) promissory notes are easily liquidated by endorsement;
(2) required stamp duty is less than on a loan agreement;
(3) upon maturity, mere presentment is sufficient to receive payment; and
(4) summary proceedings to enforce a promissory note are available.

Discounting promissory notes (*tegata-waribiki*)

The next issue is the discounting of promissory notes. Legally, the discounting of notes is regarded as the sale of notes. Since the economic function of note discounting is similar to that of a loan, banks do not invariably consent to discount notes but rather carefully check the financial status of the issuer and the holder requesting the discount.

With good customers, however, a bank will often set a ceiling for discounting of notes and agree to discount any note at the request of the customer so long as the total outstanding is below the ceiling.

Banks always insist on an executed Standard Agreement on Bank Transactions before they discount notes. When the financial status of either issuer or requestor deteriorates substantially, a bank can exercise the right to demand repurchase of the notes based on Article 6 of the Bank Transaction Agreement. This right gives the bank better protection than the protection afforded by the right of recourse on the notes, for which various presentment and notice requirements must be met by the holder. Furthermore, while the payment of the note and delivery (or return) of the note will occur simultaneously in the event of recourse on the note, payment must come first in the case where the Bank exercises its right to demand repurchase. Moreover, while the right of recourse on the note is statute-barred after one year, a five year statute of limitation applies to the bank's right to demand repurchase.

Clearing house rules

Collection of notes and cheques is done through authorised clearing houses, of which there are about 200 located around Japan. The Japanese clearing house system may be distinguished by its use of the practice of suspension of transactions with banks.

When a note or cheque is dishonoured, the bank holding it for collection prepares a report of dishonour and submits it to the clearing house. The reasons for dishonour are classified in three categories. The first is dishonour for insufficient funds or lack of an account with the bank, both of which are serious reasons. The second is dishonour for breach of contract, fraud, loss, theft, forgery, altering the seal impression, using a different method of writing the amount, using different note or cheque paper. The third is dishonour for ordinary defects of form. If dishonour is for the third reason, no report of dishonour is submitted to the clearing house, however, if it is for the first or second reason, the bank submits a report to the clearing house. In the event of dishonour for the second reason, the party whose instrument was dishonoured may lodge an objection accompanied by a deposit of the face amount with the clearing house to demonstrate that the dishonour was not due to insufficient funds. No objection is allowed to dishonour for the first reason. If the same party has another note or cheque dishonoured again within six months thereafter, he is prohibited from doing any business with banks in Japan for two years which is virtually the equivalent of going bankrupt.

Negotiable instruments are governed in Japan by two statutes: Law on Bills (Law No 20, 1932) and the Law on Cheques (Law No 57, 1933).

The Law on Bills covers both bills of exchange (*kawase tegata*) and promissory notes (*yakosoku tegata*).

Japan is one of the signatories to the Uniform Convention on Bills and Notes of 1930 (Geneva Convention). Both Laws are therefore generally in accordance with the Uniform Convention.

In general, (i) a promissory note is a means of granting a credit to the relevant obligor, (ii) a bill of exchange is a means of collection, and (iii) a cheque is a means of payment.

I.   BILLS OF EXCHANGE

A draws a bill of exchange which directs B to pay a sum of money to C. B is bound by the obligation stated on the bill only if B accepts it, ie, places his signature or seal in a certain column as an acceptor.

This sort of instrument is not commonly used in domestic transactions, but rather in import-export trades, eg, L/C, D/P and D/A.

1. Issuance

Under Article 1 of the Law on Bills, the issue of a bill of exchange must satisfy the following requirements:

(1) The term 'bill of exchange' must be embodied in the instrument.

(2) The amount of money must be specified. If the bill is payable at sight or at a fixed time after sight, the drawer may state that the sum payable is to bear

interest. In this case, the rate of interest must be specified on the face of the bill. If there is any discrepancy between the amount payable as expressed in words and in figures, the sum written in words is the sum to be paid. If a discrepancy arises from the fact that the sum payable is expressed more than once either in words or in figures, the smaller sum is the sum payable.

(3) The name of the drawee, who may be the drawer himself, must be included in the bill of exchange.

(4) The date of maturity of the instrument must be stated as being one of the following: payable at sight; at a fixed time after sight; at a fixed time after date; or at a fixed date. In Japan the maturity date is a fixed date on most bills of exchange and promissory notes.

(5) The place of payment must be stated on the bill of exchange. According to Japanese case law, this is interpreted to mean the smallest independent administrative area (a city, town, ward or village). However, the requirement of a stated place of payment has not been strictly enforced, and it suffices that the place of payment be indicated with reasonable clarity. If the place of payment is not described, it shall be the place described beside the name of the drawer, or his place of residence.

(6) The name of the payee must be stated.

(7) The date and place of issue must be stated.

(8) The signature of the issuer must be included. If there are joint issuers then they will be jointly and severally liable to the holder.

2. Acceptance

A drawee is not bound to pay until and unless he accepts the bill. Upon acceptance, the drawee-acceptor becomes bound just like the issuer of a promissory note. The drawee accepts a bill of exchange by writing the word 'accepted' or a term having a similar meaning on the bill. The drawee's signature or seal on the face of a bill is regarded as sufficient to constitute acceptance. A bill of exchange may be presented to the drawee for acceptance. A time bill may be discounted (negotiated) by ascertaining that the drawee is prepared to accept the bill. If, however, the drawee refuses to accept the bill, the holder in a chain of negotiation may immediately claim the amount of the bill from the drawer or any endorser.

II.   PROMISSORY NOTES

A promissory note is an unconditional promise in writing to pay (as opposed to an 'IOU') a certain sum.

Promissory notes are frequently used in commercial transactions among industrial companies. A bank may also often require that a borrower issue a promissory note in its favour as collateral for a bank loan.

1. Issuance

Under Article 75 of the Law on Bills, the issue of a promissory note must satisfy the following requirements:

(1) The term 'promissory note' must be embodied in the instrument.
(2) The amount of money must be specified.
(3) The date of maturity must be stated as in the case of a bill of exchange.
(4) The note must mention the place for payment.
(5) The note must include the name of the person to whose order payment is to be made.
(6) The date and place of issue must be stated.
(7) The note must be signed (or affixed with a seal) by the maker.

Upon issuance of the note, the issuer becomes primarily liable thereupon. In practice, makers do not usually sign notes. Instead, they use a registered seal (*inkan*). Article 82 of the Law on Bills provides that for the purposes of the Act the term 'signature' includes the name of a party written by another, verified by the seal of the former. Therefore, the bank must exercise care in confirming that the seal impression actually appearing on any agreement is identical to the impression of the registered seal.

2. Maturity

There are the following four types of maturity:

(1) Fixed date.
(2) At sight.
(3) Fixed term after sight.
(4) Fixed term after fixed date.

In practice, virtually all notes have a fixed date maturity.

3. Effective statement

Though not necessary, certain statements are effective if written on the note.

(1) Statement concerning interest. Such statement is effective only if the note matures either at sight or at a fixed term after sight.
(2) Statement restrictive upon endorsement.
(3) Statement indicating the instrument is 'not to order'.
(4) Statement releasing its holder from the need to draw up a protest of non-acceptance or non-payment.

4. Ineffective statements

The following statements are ineffective in and of themselves, though they do not void the instrument as a whole:

(1) Penalty clause whose rate exceeds the limit provided in the Interest Rate Restriction Law
(2) Statement waiving presentment
(3) Statement that the note shall not be collected.

5. Detrimental statements

Statements contrary to the essential nature of a negotiable instrument, such as prescribing payment by instalment or setting up conditions on the obligation to pay, are known as 'detrimental terms' and they have the effect of voiding the instrument as a whole.

6. Endorsements

(1) GENERAL

An endorsement is made on the back of the instrument by naming the endorsee or by a blank endorsement. A conditional endorsement is invalid though it does not void the instrument as a whole.

(2) LEGAL EFFECT

Endorsement is recognised as having the following three legal effects:

 (i) Transfer of title
(ii) Guarantee
(iii) Qualification as a holder (if an uninterrupted series of endorsements is established).

   An endorser not only transfers the right to the instrument to the endorsee, but also guarantees payment in case of default by the maker or any previous endorser(s), and gives the endorsee the status of holder.

7. Special endorsement

(1) An endorsement whereby the endorser does not guarantee payment
(2) An endorsement prohibiting further endorsements
(3) An endorsement for collection
(4) An endorsement in pledge
(5) Circular endorsement
(6) Endorsement after maturity: An endorsement after maturity made subsequent to a protest for nonpayment, or after the time fixed for drawing up the protest, operates only as an ordinary assignment.

8. Guarantee of payment (*tegata hoshou*)

Payment of the instrument may be guaranteed by placing the signature (of a third person) on the instrument itself. In the existence of a defect in form, the guarantor is not released by reason of invalidity of the liability he has guaranteed. If the guarantor pays the instrument, he acquires the rights arising therefrom against the person guaranteed and any persons liable to him.

9. Presentment for payment

A holder must make presentment for payment to preserve his rights. In practice, a holder brings the instrument to his bank (by way of endorsement for collection) and the bank presents the instrument for payment at a clearing house. The term for presentment is two business days following the maturity date. Consequently, a holder should endorse the instrument for collection well in advance of the maturity date, especially when the payor bank is in a remote location.

10. Legal defences

(1) REAL DEFENCES

The following defences are effective against anyone:

(i) forgery, incapacity or lack of authority as agent
(ii) failure to meet statutory requirement, time barred, maturity date not yet arrived, payment already made.

(2) PERSONAL DEFENCES

The following defences are effective only against certain persons:

(i) theft by the holder may be asserted as a defence by any party to the instrument
(ii) a defect in the underlying transactions may be effectively asserted as a defence only if the person so asserting and the holder have a direct relationship in the underlying transaction.

A holder who has knowingly acted to the detriment of the debtor when acquiring the instrument, however, may not claim that any personal defence be cut off.

11. Bona fide holder

If, for example, a negotiable instrument has been acquired by theft and then endorsed to a bona fide holder, such instrument will be deemed effectively acquired by the bona fide holder, provided that there exists an uninterrupted chain of endorsements and that the bona fide holder has not been grossly negligent.

12. Clearing house regulations

If a maker or issuer has a negotiable instrument dishonoured two or more times due to reasons such as insufficient funds or lack of an account with the bank, such maker/issuer shall be suspended from transactions with any bank in Japan.

III. CHEQUES

1. Issuance

A validly issued cheque must indicate the following items:

(1) cheque title and/or the term 'cheque' embodied in the instrument;
(2) the amount of money. In case there is a discrepancy between the amount expressed in numerals and that expressed in words, the latter shall control. In case the amount is mentioned twice or more in numerals, any discrepancy is settled in favour of the smallest amount;
(3) the name of the drawee (bank);
(4) the place of payment;
(5) the date of issue;
(6) the place of issue; and
(7) the signature of the drawer.

2. Kinds of cheques

(1) Payable to Bearer. The most common type of cheque is one payable to bearer. Such a cheque can be transferred by delivery only.
(2) Payable to named person.
(3) Payable to order. In both (2) and (3), an endorsement is necessary for payee to receive the cheque money.

3. Presentment for payment

Presentment for payment must be made within ten days of the issuance date (as written on the cheque). However, in practice, banks usually honour cheques presented later than that if presentment occurs within one month or so, unless the payor bank has been given a cancellation of order to pay (ie stop payment order).

   In practice, presentment of a cheque will usually be made at the clearing house on the day following the day the cheque is delivered to the bank for collection. If the cheque is honoured, the money will be deposited into the payee's account the day after the day of presentment.

4. Crossed cheques

In practice, most cheques are crossed on the face with a word 'Bank', in which event the payor bank may cash it only when the holder (payee) is a customer of the bank; therefore, it is unlikely that a thief will receive cash against a crossed cheque. Needless to say, this system is used for reasons of security.

5. Post-dated cheques

A cheque is sometimes issued with a future date indicated as the date of issuance. Such a cheque is called a post-dated cheque. Although the payee may present such a cheque immediately and cash it, he may be subject to a damage claim from the issuer based on a breach of contract.

6. Cancellation of order to pay

The issuer may, as of legal right, cancel the order to the bank to pay only after the term for presentment (ten days) has expired. Before the end of the ten days, however, the issuer may not compel the bank to suspend payment on the cheque even if the cheque is lost or stolen.

In practice, however, banks usually suspend payment voluntarily because the bank will not be liable to the payee (holder) in any event.

II.   Securities and Exchange Law

The Japanese Securities Dealers' Association

Takahira Ogawa
Nikko Research Center Limited

1. Roles of the JSDA and the Ministry of Finance

The Japanese Securities Dealers Association (JSDA) is registered with the Ministry of Finance as the only 'self-regulatory organisation which consists of securities firms under the provisions of the Securities and Exchange Law, and the Law on Foreign Securities Firms'. (Article 67 of the Securities and Exchange Law, Rule 3 of the JSDA Rules.) Although it is a voluntary non-profit making organisation, all licensed securities firms are members of the JSDA.

The importance of the JSDA lies both in its membership and in its role in working with the Ministry of Finance to provide a regulatory framework for the secondary markets of the Japanese securities industry. At the Ministry of Finance the Securities Bureau is responsible for the securities industry, covering not only securities firms whose activities are broking, dealing, and underwriting, but also fund management companies, and investment trust and management companies. The Securities Bureau carefully scrutinises each securities firm's policies, procedures, financial condition, and other important information related to its activities.

This ministerial surveillance is based on the Securities and Exchange Law, the Law on Foreign Securities Firms and other laws such as company law and the Commercial Code that influence corporate activities. But the provisions of these laws are too general and not precise enough to give clear guidance for a great deal of the daily activities of securities firms. Accordingly, the Ministry of Finance relies on the JSDA to provide the detailed regulations needed to achieve fair and smooth trading, to protect small investors and to promote the sound development of the securities industry.

2. Organisation

As of March 1987, the membership of the JSDA comprised 257 firms of which 36 were foreign securities firms. Representatives of these firms meet at a General

Assembly, which is convened for the making of 'supreme decisions', such as changing the JSDA's constitution, adopting a budget and setting accounts.

Under the General Assembly, there is a Board of Directors which deliberate on important matters regarding the general management and supervision of the Association's affairs. The board consists of 30 directors from member firms and up to five standing directors. In addition, there are five auditors from member firms and one standing auditor who can also attend board meetings.

Acting closely with the Board of Directors is the Central Council, which advises the Chairman of the JSDA on important matters that can affect the management of the Association.

The JSDA has five standing committees. These are the General Affairs, Business Conduct, Policy, Treasury, and Training Committees. In addition various special committees can be set up when required by the Board of Directors. If necessary, sub-committees or advisory committees can be set up under the standing committees or special committees.

The Disciplinary Committee provides, at the Chairman's request, advice and regulations regarding the member firms, their executives and their employees.

The JSDA also has ten district offices and affiliate committees such as the Registered Representative Qualification Committee, the Urgent Financing Deliberation Committee and the Central Arbitration Committee.

3. Regulations

The JSDA was established to achieve the 12 goals listed in the Appendix to this chapter, which include the maintenance of fair trading practices and the enhancement of public faith. In order to achieve these goals, the JSDA has established the following rules.

There are four main types of rules which support the Securities and Exchange Law and form the backbone of the practical regulatory framework. These are (1) Rules on OTC Markets, covering both equity and bond quotations and transactions, (2) Rules on Foreign Securities Transactions, (3) Uniform Practice Codes and Dispute Settlement Rules, and (4) other rules concerning such matters as customer solicitation and client relations, securities industry employees, advertising, safe keeping of securities, etc.

The OTC Markets Rules may be divided into those concerning equities and those concerning bonds. As regards equities, if a company's shares are quoted on one or more stock exchanges, then transactions cannot be made outside the stock exchanges on which they are quoted. This system is derived from 'the principle of concentrated trading in the stock exchanges'. In special cases it is possible to sell outside the stock exchanges, but forward notices to the relevant stock exchanges are required and such trading has to be done in accordance with stock exchange regulations. Accordingly, the OTC Market Rules only regulate equity trading on the OTC markets (which are comparable to the USM in the United Kingdom) and do not impinge at all on trading on the Japanese stock exchanges.

On the other hand, the OTC Markets Rules are very relevant to bond transactions since the majority are done in the OTC markets. Although some government bonds are quoted on the Tokyo Stock Exchange (TSE), their trading volumes are very small compared with the estimated total bond trading volumes in the OTC markets.

Until recently, there has only been a negligible amount of transactions in the foreign section of the TSE. From the second half of 1985 the volume of transactions picked up quite dramatically, due to a rush in listing foreign companies shares on the TSE and the globalisation of portfolio management of Japanese institutional investors.

As a result it has become increasingly important that foreign listings and transactions on the foreign section be properly regulated. To this end the JSDA has promulgated its Foreign Securities Transactions Rules. However, adequate regulation can be achieved only when differences in various market practices, of different countries concerning such matters as accounting principles and corporate strategies, are resolved. As yet there has been no real discussion of these matters between the stock exchanges of London, New York and Tokyo. Still, the three exchanges have begun to co-operate on the problem of insider trading and this is seen as the first step towards harmonisation.

The JSDA has two sets of Uniform Practice Codes, the Code for Resolution of Problems arising from OTC Transactions, and the Code for Disposal of Rights in cases where Stock Transfers are forgotten.

There are two sets of dispute settlement rules, the Rules for Arbitration and Settlement of Disputes between Members and Customers, and the Rules for Arbitration of Disputes between Members.

In addition to the above rules and regulations, the JSDA has issued regulations covering such matters as qualification examinations for registered representatives, the provision of special financing to members firms, and the inspection of the business and financial condition of member firms.

4. Comparison of two regulatory frameworks

The Japanese regulatory system for its securities markets is very similar to that of the United Kingdom in the context of using self-regulatory organisations and, in actual fact, the JSDA has functions similar to those of The Securities Association (TSA) in the United Kingdom. However, on closer comparison there are many differences between the two systems. For example, in Japan the influence of the Ministry of Finance is very strong despite the JSDA's existence. On the other hand, in the United Kingdom the Department of Trade and Industry has given its statutory power to the Securities and Investments Board (the SIB), which is not a government office but a voluntary association.

One of the most significant differences is that there is no obligation to become a member of the JSDA in order to conduct a securities business, while in the United Kingdom a securities firm is required to become a member of TSA or alternatively to make a direct application to the SIB.

Although there would be many disadvantages (mainly cost disadvantages) if a securities firm were not to become a member of the JSDA, it is nonetheless possible to stay out of the JSDA and conduct a securities business since there is no legal requirement for membership. However, in practice because the regulatory structure of Japanese securities firms depends on the self-regulatory system of the JSDA, the Ministry of Finance would not permit securities firms to do business without being members of the JSDA.

Historically, it is worth mentioning that at the time of the major shakeout of Japanese securities markets in 1965, when it was decided that all securities firms needed a licence issued by the Ministry, it was argued that compulsory membership of the JSDA was necessary in order to maintain compliance and ensure the sound financial condition of securities firms. However, no decision was made, and since then there has been virtually no discussion on this matter.

Appendix

THE GOALS OF THE JAPANESE
SECURITIES DEALERS' ASSOCIATION

JSDA was set up in order to achieve the following goals:

(1) To promote compliance by member firms of regulations relating to the industry and to maintain order among member firms.

(2) To enhance public faith in securities transactions by encouraging fair industry practices and by maintaining the integrity and credibility of member firms.

(3) To increase the efficiency in the management of the stock market in Japan by establishing uniform procedures and standards for member firms relating to securities transactions.

(4) To facilitate communication and the resolution of differing views among member firms.

(5) To inspect the business and financial conditions of member firms.

(6) To assist in resolving disputes arising from transactions either between investors and member firms or between the member firms themselves.

(7) To provide training, recognition, and awards to officers and employees of member firms so as to improve their competence and to conduct qualification examinations for registered representatives.

(8) To conduct research and studies on problems relating to securities and the securities markets and, when necessary, to present recommendations to the government.

(9) To educate the public about securities and the securities markets.

(10) To facilitate communication and co-operation between the association and other organisations concerned with the securities industry.

(11) To provide financing to member firms or to guarantee their obligations in the event of management difficulties resulting from natural disasters or unforeseen circumstances.

(12) To conduct operations necessary for achieving the above-stated goals of the Association.

Japanese corporate financing through domestic and foreign securities markets

Takahira Ogawa
Nikko Research Center Limited

1. The current situation

Lately, the number of Japanese debenture issues in the euro market has grown rapidly. This is partly because of deregulation in issuing eurobonds (including euroyen bonds) but also because of the relative rigidity and inefficiency of the domestic primary market. This chapter is concerned with the main factors which have inhibited and continue to impede the development of the domestic primary debentures market.[1]

In Japan, the primary market in non-equity related debentures is not very active. Utility companies, the recently privatised Nippon Telephone and Telegraph (NTT) and public corporations are the main users of straight debentures as a source to finance their huge demand for money. However, it is rare for industrial and commercial companies to issue straight bonds. Also most of the banks and all the securities firms are prohibited from making such issues.

On the other hand, there are fewer restrictions on issues of equity related bonds (convertible bonds and bonds with equity warrants) and these products have become much more popular than issues of both straight bonds and shares. In fact, share issues have declined because companies have found it cheaper to issue convertible bonds and bonds with equity warrants. Even so, restrictions which still remain have no parallel in other leading financial markets.

2. Legal structure and its background

The major laws and regulations that govern the scope and terms of the domestic debenture primary market include the Securities and Exchange Law, the Commercial Code, the Secured Debenture Trust Law and the Law on the Provisional Measures concerning the Limits on the amounts of Debentures.[2]

---

[1] For details, see chapters 5 & 6 of A. Viner, *Inside Japan's Financial Markets* (London, 1987).
[2] Currently, reforms of laws concerning debentures are being discussed. It is proposed primarily by securities companies and *Keidanren* (Japan Economic Organisations Association), inter alia, to remove the limits on the amount of debentures to be issued.

Most of the practical regulations covering the domestic debenture primary market are made by agreement between the Bond Underwriters Association of Japan (BUAJ) and the 'Big Four' securities firms (Nomura, Nikko, Daiwa and Yamaichi) and those 'agreements' are usually made under the influence of the Ministry of Finance. In addition, the Securities and Exchange Council, an advisory organisation attached to the Ministry of Finance, sometimes plays an important role, especially when the regulatory system itself has to be revised.

3. Straight debentures

The number of companies with unredeemed straight bonds at the end of March 1976 was 259, but by March 1985 that number had declined dramatically to 155 companies. If issues by electricity companies are excluded, from April 1985 to March 1986, there were only ten new issues of straight debentures, and these included issues by the Nippon Broadcasting Corporation (NHK) and the Municipal Express Railways Board. In view of the massive growth in eurobond issues from the latter half of 1984, it is quite obvious that the Japanese companies have progressively lost interest in issuing straight debentures in the domestic market.

Several opinion polls have been compiled by the BUAJ to discover the reasons why companies have moved away from the domestic debenture market. The results of the 1985 poll, which covered 396 companies and included those which had just issued domestic debentures, indicate the reasons quite clearly. The following summary of their responses shows that one third complained about such problems as the requirement for secured assets and the considerable expenses involved:

(1) Other financial methods such as issuing convertibles or shares are more interesting   67.7%

(2) Issuing procedures such as providing secured assets are very troublesome   38.1%

(3) The domestic market is more expensive than issuing foreign currency denominated straight debentures, such as eurodollar bonds   34.8%

(4) Basically, issues on the domestic market require secured assets   33.8%

(5) Companies cannot issue quickly enough to take advantage of the best interest levels at the time   26.3%

(6) The domestic straight debenture market is more expensive than borrowing   24.5%

(7) There is no demand for money, which is essential for the successful issue of debentures   11.9%

4. Obstacles to issuing domestic straight debentures

More than a third of the companies which responded to the 1985 poll complained of the need for secured assets as a prerequisite to debenture issues.

Since 1933, when trustees agreed to refuse any issue of debentures without secured assets, it has been impossible to issue unsecured debentures. However, in 1979 the BUAJ published a 'Report on Unsecured Debentures' and raised the possibility of issuing unsecured debentures. But, under the self-regulation requirements which were still regarded as necessary in the Report, the possible issuers were restricted to two companies, Matsushita Electronics and Toyota Motor Company. And even they could not issue unsecured debentures because of the lack of administrative procedures needed to fulfill the requirement of financial fitness, as stipulated by the rule.

In January 1985, TDK was the first private company to issue unsecured straight debentures in compliance with the new procedures on financial fitness introduced in December 1984. These procedures were introduced following an agreement between the BUAJ and the 'Big Four' and contained restrictions concerning secured assets, self capitalisation ratios and dividends. After those restrictions were relaxed in October 1985, the total number of companies which were able to issue unsecured straights increased to 63 by the end of October 1986. By March 1987 the number of eligible companies had doubled. Still, however, the vast majority of eligible companies can issue straight debentures only on a secured basis.

The domestic market is also hampered by restrictions on redemption procedures. Until October 1983, no debenture could be redeemed at once at the end of its maturity. Rather, the regulations of the BUAJ required each debenture to be redeemed at a fixed proportion in each year, with the redemption beginning after a fixed period calculated on the basis of the debenture's maturity. This is called the 'constant portion redemption system'. However, in October 1983, the regulation was amended so that debentures with six or seven year maturities could be issued without such restrictions. And, since October 1985, debentures with 10 or 12 year maturities can be issued provided certain conditions are fulfilled.

Until the latter half of the 1980s Japan has witnessed very rigid yield movements in its domestic bond market. For example, from April 1950 to October 1955 there was no change of yield on newly issued debentures, and only six changes during the next ten years. The reasons for this inflexibility were as follows.

In the past, the conditions of each debenture issue, such as the coupon rate and issue price, were set in accordance with guidelines determined by the underwriting consortium. The members of this consortium were lead managers (securities houses) and trustees (banks). There was no participation by the borrowers and the guidelines were decided upon consideration of such factors as government bond yields and long-term prime interest rates. Obviously, this process of deciding yield on issue did not always reflect prevailing market conditions and the differences between issuing companies.

This system was changed in 1984. Since then an underwriting consortium meets each month to decide the issue yields for each credit rating of debentures.

Furthermore, from the beginning of 1987, the so-called 'competing underwriting system' was introduced, as a result of which borrowers can now choose their lead managers at the time they receive offers of underwriting conditions. Also, it is now possible to choose issue timing whereas before 1987 it was always at the end of the month.

Finally, there have always been complaints about the long and tiresome issuing procedures in the domestic debenture market. Borrowers have to do a lot of paper work to satisfy the requirements of the Ministry of Finance. In the past it took three to four months to finalise an issuing schedule. Nowadays, it takes about one and a half months to complete an issue.

5. Convertible bonds

The latter half of the 1980s has witnessed considerable progress in the development of the primary convertible bond market. The most important structural change followed the revision of the Commercial Code in April 1974. Before that, any company which hoped to issue convertible bonds had to call a general meeting of shareholders to obtain their agreement to the conditions of the issue, such as the total amount of issue, the conversion price, the period within which investors would have the right to convert and the type of shares the company could issue on conversion. Since the Code's revision, companies no longer have to obtain shareholder approval except when the convertible bonds are to be issued only to non-shareholders with an advantageous conversion price. If this exception does not apply, the issue of convertible bonds can be approved by the company's board of directors (Art 296 Commercial Code).

As with straight bond issues, issues of convertible bonds have benefitted from the relaxation of the secured asset requirements and the improved flexibility of issue yields. In the past, convertible bond yields were very high and, since no consideration was given to the fact that CB's had the merit of being convertible into shares, borrowers had to pay the same coupon rate as for straight bonds.

6. Bonds with warrants

Following the revision of the Commercial Code in 1981, Japanese companies have been able to issue bonds with equity warrants. In 1981 three companies issued this type of bond. However, in September that year the Board of Directors of the Japanese Securities Dealers' Association decided to prohibit all issues of bonds with detachable warrants. This resolution was passed because the JSDA thought the introduction of detachable warrants would upset the market. It was believed that Japanese investors were not sufficiently familiar with trading detachable warrants and that detachable warrants might cause share prices to fluctuate. In November 1985 this resolution was abolished, and since then it has been possible to issue and trade bonds with detachable warrants.

The current regulations for issuing bonds with warrants are much the same as those for convertible bonds, because they are regarded as having the same characteristics.

7. The major obstacles to further improvements

The changes mentioned above have led to significant improvements in the domestic primary market, the latest revisions having been made by the Ministry of Finance in November 1986 following a report of the Advisory Committee on Securities and Exchange, but the need for further change still remains. Perhaps the most important barrier is the fairly rigid interest rate structure prevailing in Japan. Any change to this structure will depend on governmental policy, but its retention will continue to limit the domestic financial market's efficiency and attractiveness as compared with other leading financial markets.

8. Shares

There are some unique requirements imposed on the making of public offers of shares at market price in Japan. First, if a company makes a public offer of shares at market price then, within a certain period of time, it has to re-distribute the premium it receives either by an increased cash dividend or by a stock dividend. This rule was originally decided in 1965 by the 'Controlling Organisation of Increasing Shareholders' Capital', which consisted of the Ministry of Finance, the Bank of Japan, the 'Big Four' securities firms and the major banks, and took the form of the 'Private Rule Concerning Handling of Capital Increases'.

In April 1972, underwriting managers of the 'Big Four' securities firms met and decided to introduce a replacement code. The code was revised in February 1973 to make it more practical and since then, although there have been some minor changes, the basic framework has not been changed. At the same meeting the 'Agreement concerning Convertible Bonds' was decided to standardise issues of convertibles with share issues at market price.

Currently, premiums may be re-distributed to shareholders in one of three ways: first, by increasing the cash dividend; secondly, by making a new issue of bonus shares; and thirdly, by a combination of the former two methods. If a company chooses the first method, then it must re-distribute about 25% of the premium it receives from a public offer of shares at market price. The second option requires the company to pay back more than 15% of the premium through issuing bonus shares within two years after the public issue, and a total of more than 20% of the premium by the time of its next public offer. The third option requires that 15% of the premium be paid back as bonus shares within two years of the public offer and that a better cash dividend level than before be maintained.

This code was made in order to protect shareholders' rights, but some argument exists as to its theoretical basis. Some commentators argue that since shareholders own a company, any premium that it makes from a public offering of shares or convertible bonds at market price is owned by the original shareholders and should be redistributed to them. Others argue that by requiring the company to announce its schedule of re-distribution of premiums, the code reduces the impact that a public issue might otherwise have on the price of the company's shares and, accordingly, benefits the shareholders and the market. These arguments are not convincing. Shareholder pre-emption rights could be adequately protected by each company amending its articles of association in whatever way it chooses, rather than by relying on a code to provide protection for all companies. As it stands the code restricts the corporate finance techniques available throughout the Japanese market.

9. Euro and foreign bond issues

Thus there still remain various obstacles to financing in the domestic financial and capital markets. On the other hand, there are much easier and more cost effective markets such as the euromarket.

From the early 1960s Japanese companies started to issue eurobonds. However, until the new Foreign Exchange Law was introduced in 1980, making it easier for Japanese companies to issue foreign and eurobonds, those activities were not significant in terms of quantity. After the introduction of the new Foreign Exchange Law, deregulation of euroyen financing for Japanese companies followed in 1984.

This structural deregulation has contributed to the increase of financing activities in the euro and foreign markets. Of course, it should not be overlooked that the progress that has been made in developing new financing techniques such as swaps, euro CP, etc, in euro and other markets, all of which have helped reduce financing costs to the lowest levels. However, if the Japanese government had not deregulated this area, no Japanese companies would have been able to issue euroyen bonds. Therefore, when the vitality of the euromarket is compared with the Japanese domestic market, the importance of continued deregulation is obvious.

(100 million yen)

Year	Convertible Bonds		Straight Bonds		Bonds with Warrants		New Share Issues		Total	
	Domestic	Overseas	Domestic	Overseas	Domestic	Overseas	Domestic	Overseas	Domestic	Overseas
1978	27/ 2,770	81/ 4,321	153/ 13,133	21/ 1,305	—	—	250/ 10,329	2/ 134	430/ 26,232	104/ 5,760
1979	31/ 3,535	91/ 5,640	126/ 12,981	30/ 1,870	—	—	253/ 6,605	4/ 148	410/ 23,121	125/ 7,658
1980	12/ 965	73/ 5,171	101/ 9,935	38/ 1,836	—	—	256/ 11,601	13/ 1,077	369/ 22,501	124/ 8,804
1981	52/ 5,260	132/ 10,325	127/ 12,690	10/ 528	3/ 200	5/ 448	285/ 17,932	24/ 2,874	467/ 36,082	171/ 14,170
1982	46/ 4,175	78/ 6,323	91/ 10,475	97/ 6,810	9/ 470	9/ 662	172/ 10,154	11/ 626	318/ 25,274	195/ 14,421
1983	67/ 8,610	159/ 11,998	62/ 6,830	65/ 4,120	3/ 170	34/ 3,253	123/ 3,494	6/ 778	258/ 24,104	264/ 20,149
1984	125/ 16,115	158/ 12,346	55/ 7,200	97/ 11,272	1/ 30	61/ 4,372	152/ 8,146	10/ 495	333/ 31,491	326/ 28,485
1985	142/ 15,855	90/ 9,530	63/ 9,345	157/ 14,366	5/ 550	93/ 8,820	131/ 6,513	2/ 107	341/ 32,353	342/ 32,824
1986	204/ 34,680	49/ 4,894	61/ 9,800	204/ 18,765	11/ 1,040	213/ 20,028	110/ 8,315	1/ 6	386/ 51,835	467/ 43,693
1987	302/ 50,550	93/ 10,846	27/ 9,150	87/ 10,104	—	234/ 34,715	149/ 20,839	1/ 303	478/ 80,539	420/ 55,968
1988 March	51/ 7,795	24/ 2,036	11/ 2,800	17/ 1,826	—	49/ 6,401	47/ 4338	—	109/ 14,932	90/ 10,263

Provided by courtesy of the Nomura Research Institute (editors)

Recent developments in the Securities and Exchange Law in Japan

Osamu Karihara
General Manager
IBJ International

I. Disclosure

1. BASIC STRUCTURE OF DISCLOSURE REQUIREMENT

The disclosure system was introduced into the Japanese capital market when the Securities and Exchange Law[1] was enacted in 1948 following securities regulations in the United States. At first, it was not a familiar concept not only for ordinary investors but also professionals. However, with the growth of the Japanese capital market, disclosure has become one of the key measures of investor protection.

In Japan there is another important disclosure requirement under the Commercial Code.[2] Private corporations are required to send reports on business and financial conditions to the shareholders before the regular shareholders meeting. The aim of this disclosure system is to provide necessary information to shareholders. Therefore, the beneficiaries of disclosed information are different from those under the disclosure required by the Securities and Exchange Law.

There are three basic disclosure requirements under the Securities and Exchange Law [see Appendix]:

(1) Disclosure at the public offering of securities. The filing of the Securities Registration Statement is necessary before offering for sale and solicitation for purchase. Prospectuses must be furnished to investors when sales efforts are made.

(2) Issuers of (a) publicly offered securities where a Securities Registration

---

[1] An English translation of the Securities and Exchange Law, Law on Foreign Securities Firms, and the Securities Investment Trust Law can be found in Japan Securities Research Institute, ed, *Japanese Securities Laws* (Tokyo, 1987). See also L. Loss, M. Yazawa & B. Banoff, *Japanese Securities Regulation* (Tokyo, 1983).

[2] Japanese Institute of Certified Accountants, ed, *Corporate Disclosure in Japan* (Tokyo, 1984 & 1987).

Statement has been filed, (b) listed securities on a stock exchange, or (c) securities registered for quotation with a Securities Dealers Association in Japan, are required to file a Securities Report for each of the financial periods and also required to file Semi-Annual Reports, which are simpler than the Securities Reports. Those reports or copies are kept on file at certain places such as the Ministry of Finance, stock exchanges and the Securities Dealers Association. They are also published by the Government Printing Office. It is not always easy for ordinary investors to read and analyse those documents by themselves. However, it is quite useful for institutional investors, rating agencies, analysts and journalists. Through those channels, information about issuers can be delivered to the public.

(3) Disclosure in the process of a takeover bid. Those who want to start a takeover bid have to file with the Ministry of Finance in advance. This disclosure requirement was introduced when the Securities and Exchange Law was amended in 1971.

2. PROPOSED CHANGES IN THE DISCLOSURE SYSTEM

As the capital market grows and Japanese corporations float securities more frequently, some changes are generally considered necessary in the present disclosure system. Two different aspects of the recent discussions should be noted. One is the need for simplification of the disclosure procedure. Issuers and underwriters require shortening of the filing period in order to avoid the risk of market volatility. Issuers also demand simplification of the forms of the Securities Registration Statement and prospectus.

The other aspect is the need for more information. As activities of corporations become more diversified and internationalised, investors and analysts require more detailed and sophisticated information.

The Advisory Committee on Securities Exchange, which is an advisory committee to the Minister of Finance, recently proposed changes in the disclosure requirement. To pick up some important proposals, the first and most noteworthy one is the introduction of a similar system to 'Shelf Registration' in the United States. Once a company has filed with the Ministry of Finance, within a certain period it can come to the market without further filing. This system is expected to enhance flexibility of flotation of securities.

The second proposal of the Advisory Committee is the shortening of the waiting period in the filing procedure. Under the current regulatory system the Securities Registration Statement becomes effective upon expiration of 30 days after its filing. Although this period may be shortened by one week in certain cases at the discretion of the Ministry of Finance, it is still considered a bit too long in the recent changeable market. Therefore, it is proposed that the waiting period may be reduced to 15 days through the extension of discretionary capacity at the Ministry of Finance.

Thirdly, the need for more sophisticated information was discussed. The Advisory Committee proposed:

(a) Consolidated financial statements should be presented as a one-month allowance after the submission of Securities Reports. Explanation of corporate group activities should be attached to consolidated financial statements, too.

(b) Detailed cash flow tables should be included in the Securities Report.

(c) Segmental reporting is proposed. Under the present disclosure system, sales results by product and export results by major products are the only segmental information. No segmental reporting about profit and loss is required. Corporations are generally reluctant to disclose segmental information because of concern about its detrimental effect upon competitiveness and the burden of producing it. However, the Council pointed out that further development in segmental reporting is preferable and asked the administration to study feasible methods.

Editors' note: The Diet—Japanese Parliament—passed a bill amending the Securities and Exchange Law in May 1988. Proposals of the Advisory Committee are now incorporated in the Law.

II.   Insider trading

If unfair use of insider information proliferates, it will be destructive to the confidence of the public in the capital market. Although there exists a general notion against insider trading in Japan, almost no legal action has been brought against insider trading since the Securities and Exchange Law was enacted. This does not mean that insider trading did not take place in the Japanese market. Rather, it appears that current regulations are not sufficient to sustain legal action against it.

The Securities and Exchange Law has a provision, Art 58, which generally prohibits the use of manipulative and deceptive devices in transactions of securities. This provision was modelled on s 10 (b) of the Securities Exchange Act 1934 in the United States. Although extensive and detailed case law has developed in the United States under the provision of the Securities Exchange Act, there has been no similar development in Japan. This is mainly due to the fact that under the traditional Japanese legal practice, it is not easy to impose criminal sanctions in insider trading cases under Art 58 because its expression is fairly general and not specific to insider trading. For this reason the Ministry of Finance has been reluctant to use Art 58 for prosecuting. Rather the government has required proper conduct of intermediaries: directors and employees of securities companies are prohibited from selling or purchasing securities using inside information.

Article 189 deals with a specific form of insider trading. That is, if directors or major shareholders of a company get capital gain in the short-term (ie within six months) in the transaction of the shares of the company, the company has the right to ask them to return the profit to the company. Moreover, if the company does not take this action, shareholders can request the company to do it. If the company still does not take action, after some period they can take an action on behalf of the company. This article was instituted to prevent insider trading, too. However, it is generally said that it has not been effective. When the Securities and Exchange Law was enacted, there was Art 188 which prescribed that directors and major shareholders of a company had to report their holdings and changes of shares of the company to the regulatory body. However, this article was deleted in 1953 as one of the many amendments of the Securities and Exchange Law.

Recently there have been some developments in the regulation of insider trading reflecting the international tendency for stricter control against it. The Securities Dealers Association of Japan adopted new provisions in its fair practice rules. The first one is that member companies have to try to prevent officers or major shareholders of issuing companies from selling or purchasing shares of their companies using special information obtained through their positions. Secondly, member companies have to establish in-house rules against insider trading and ensure that their staff follow them. Thirdly, securities companies are required to set up new card systems. Those who are classified as 'insiders'—directors of companies and their spouses and relatives, major shareholders, affiliated companies, etc—are to be shown on the information card. Staff of securities companies are expected to use this system to prevent insider trading.

Also, the Tokyo Stock Exchange issued a letter to listed companies in June warning that directors, major shareholders and senior staff should refrain from buying and selling their companies' shares using insider information.

These are not legal requirements but self-regulatory measures. How they will work in the Japanese market is yet to be seen, but if they prove to be ineffective, the next step will probably be introduction of some specific rules into the Securities and Exchange Law.[3]

Editors' note: The Securities and Exchange Law, as amended in May 1988, now has a detailed provision concerning the control of insider trading (Arts 190, 190–2, and 190–3). For details, see Hiroshi Oda's article in the present volume.

III.   Separation between banking and securities business

1. ENACTMENT OF ART 65

Before the Securities and Exchange Law was enacted in 1948, Japanese banks were able to engage in any kind of securities business. Under this so-called universal banking system, banks acted as major underwriters of securities, especially fixed-income securities.

When the Securities and Exchange Law was enacted, Art 65 was copied from

---

[3] The Advisory Committee on Securities and Exchange set up a sub-committee in October 1987 to study the introduction of legal measures against insider trading.

the Glass-Steagall Act in the United States, which was the beginning of the separate system. It should be noted that this change was not a natural development, but rather an importation of a different idea from abroad.

Since then the Japanese capital market has grown under this new legal framework. Banks could no longer act as underwriters of corporate securities. However, large banks, which were major players before World War II, have had a fairly big influence in the corporate bond market as commissioned banks and investors.[4] Also, it should be added that the Japanese banks are allowed to hold corporate shares within certain limits. In this sense the Japanese capital market has a characteristic of something between the separate system and the universal banking system, although legally it is almost identical to that of the United States.

2. RECENT DEVELOPMENTS IN SECURITIES' ACTIVITIES BY BANKS

In the past several years, some significant changes have taken place. First of all there was a significant change in the role of banks in the government bond market. Although banks were major members of syndicates since the resumption of government bond flotation in 1966, they refrained from distributing them to the public and from trading in the secondary market in accordance with the agreement among syndicate members. This was because the amount of government bonds was relatively small and securities companies were considered to be protected from competition with banks. However, the situation changed dramatically when the Japanese government started to float huge amounts of government bonds after the first oil crisis. Banks strongly urged their participation in the distributing and trading of government bonds in order to ease their burden of large underwriting positions. When the new Banking Law was enacted in 1981, Art 65-2 was added to the Securities and Exchange Law paving the way for banks to engage in those businesses. Banks began distribution of new issues of government bonds in 1983 and started trading in seasoned bonds in the next year. Today, banks are major players in this market as well as the big securities houses.

Secondly, banks were allowed to have special status in the Tokyo Stock Exchange when the futures market in government bonds was introduced in 1985. Banks now have a substantial share of this market as in the cash market. However, banks are not allowed to engage in brokerage activities in government bond futures, which has been one of the big disputes between the banking and securities industries.

Thirdly, there has been a significant development in private placement activities in the corporate bond market. In Japan, private placement of corporate bonds was treated only as a complementary measure to public offering. The issuing amount was restricted up to two billion yen and issuers

[4] A commissioned bank has a financial advisory function to the issuer and also has statutory and contractual rights and duties, like a trustee, to safeguard the bondholders' interests. Commissioned banks have also co-operated with securities companies in setting certain rules and practices in order to achieve steady development of the corporate bond market in Japan.

who had once come to the market through a public offering were usually required not to return to private placement. Therefore, it has been a financing measure only for medium and small corporations.

Private placement has its own advantages such as tailor-made characteristics and reduction of the burden of disclosure requirement. To activate the private placement market it was agreed to increase the issuing amount up to ten billion yen. Acting as arrangers, banks are expecting a more important role in corporate finance.

3. PRESENT ISSUES ON ART 65

Looking at these developments, one can see that banks are now more involved in capital market activities. But there are still a number of issues in relation to Art 65. One of the most important issues is the Three Bureaux Agreement which prohibits Japanese banks' overseas subsidiaries from acting as lead managers for foreign bonds of Japanese corporations.

It seems quite strange if one considers the fact that those subsidiaries, which are usually established as merchant banks under UK legislation, are allowed to carry out any sort of securities business. There is no such restriction upon the activities of subsidiaries of US commercial banks, which are under similar legal frame. The original aim of the agreement was to protect Japanese securities companies from competition with banks' subsidiaries. However, since Japanese securities companies have grown so big and strong, one can see no reason to protect them under the same measure introduced more than ten years ago. Besides, it should be pointed out that only a small number of houses can substantially enjoy the existence of this protection. In other words, this is not a problem affecting the overall securities industry which has many medium and small companies.

Also it is a noteworthy trend that some non-Japanese merchant banks recently succeeded in becoming lead managers even for euroyen bonds issued by Japanese corporations. This fact makes the Three Bureaux Agreement more unfair and irrelevant. To enhance competition and encourage innovation the agreement should be abolished immediately.

IV.   Some comments on the future direction of the Securities and Exchange Law

The Japanese financial system is now in a transitional period. Deregulation of interest rates and relaxation of various regulations have taken place and the pace has now been accelerated since the agreement of the Japan-US Yen-Dollar Committee in 1984.

Continuing growth of the capital market is expected with this trend in the whole financial market. To support the healthy development it is particularly important to provide effective measures for investors' protection. At the same time fair competition among participants in the market is also essential to enhance efficiency. From this point of view it would be worth considering whether the present securities regulations are sufficient or not.

One of the key factors of the Securities and Exchange Law is the concept of 'securities'. It sets the scope and limits in the application of the law. For example, disclosure is basically required when securities to be issued are one of those defined in Art 2 of the law. The definition of the securities companies depends on the concept of securities, too. That is, securities companies are defined as institutions which engage in selling, buying, broking, underwriting and other transactions in securities (see Arts 2 (8) and 43). Also regulations about fair transactions are applied to those of securities defined in the law.

There are some fundamental problems about the concept of securities. Firstly, the law explicitly lists types of securities. Therefore, it is impossible to apply the law to a transaction of a certain instrument unless it falls within the category of securities. Secondly, the definition in Art 2 is strictly formal, based on legal characteristics of the instruments, not on their economic functions. Thirdly, if an instrument is once defined as a security in the Securities and Exchange Law, it means that Art 65 is inevitably applied to the transactions of the instrument. In other words, if a new financial instrument is introduced and banks are expected to be intermediaries for it, it is difficult to apply the Securities and Exchange Law. As a result, its investor protection measures are not applied to transactions of that instrument.

Those problems inherent in the present law have restricted its effectiveness to a certain extent. The concept of securities should be reconsidered to cope with the new environment.

This bears on the future of Art 65.

In the United States, the Glass-Steagall Act deals not with the regulation of the securities market but with that of banking activities. It restricts the activities of commercial banks basically from a sound banking point of view. Therefore, it is rather strange to put a regulation like Art 65 among securities market regulations, which are basically intended as measures for investor protection. It should be extracted from the Securities and Exchange Law and transferred to the Banking Law.

The contents of Art 65 should be reconsidered too, because new entry of banks in corporate securities, transactions and foreign institutions is desirable to enhance the competition among intermediaries. Perhaps 'gradualism' will be suitable and practical in this matter. In other words, the first step is the entry of banks into the fixed-income market. Judging from activities and experiences of banks' subsidiaries in the eurobond market, there seems basically no problem in allowing banks to engage in the bond market of corporations and foreign institutions as underwriters and dealers. If the government thinks certain limitations on that activity are preferable from a sound banking point of view, some regulatory measures may be considered: for example, the requirement of a certain ratio of capital to underwriting positions or setting minimum standards for the credit standing of issuers.

Originally Art 65 was introduced following US legislation. However, if we think about the future legal system, we can probably formulate a new framework based upon the experience and needs of the Japanese financial system.

Appendix

The following is a brief summary of the disclosure system under the Securities and Exchange Law of Japan.

I.   The disclosure requirements for the public offering of new or outstanding securities are contained in Arts 4 & 5 of the Law. These provisions require that a Securities Registration Statement (*yūkashouken todokeidesho*) be filed by the issuer with the Ministry Of Finance (MOF). The information to be contained in the registration statement is specified in Art 5 of the Law. This statement is made available to the public at the MOF and, when the securities are listed, at the relevant Stock Exchange and the Securities Dealers Association. An exemption from this filing requirement applies where the aggregate amount of the issuing or selling value of the security is less than 100 million yen and where an exemption is prescribed by a ministerial ordinance.

Article 2(3) defines the term 'public offering of new security' under the Law as meaning 'to solicit many and unspecific persons for subscription to acquire any newly issued security under uniform terms'. Also, Art 2(4) defines 'public offering of outstanding security' as meaning 'to make an offer to many and unspecific persons to sell, or solicit such persons for subscription to buy, any already issued security under uniform terms'. In addition, a directive of the MOF has stated that any new issue of shares for an increase of capital (*zoushi*) to existing shareholders, employees, and trade partners (totalling at least 50 persons) is to be regarded as a public offering.

Under Art 8 such filing is deemed to be effective 30 days after the date of filing with the MOF. Article 15 prohibits sales of such securities by issuers, offerers, underwriters or securities companies before that effective date.

Article 13(1) requires any issuer making a public offering of new or outstanding securities subject to the above disclosure requirements to prepare a prospectus which, under Art 13(2) is to contain information based on the registration statement filed with the MOF. Under Art 15(2), such a prospectus must be delivered to each purchaser on or before the sale of any new or outstanding securities.

II.   The Securities and Exchange Law also provides for continuous or periodic disclosure, the objective being to provide adequate information both to prospective purchasers and to sellers of securities. Article 24(1) provides that a 'Periodic Securities Report' must be filed with the MOF by issuers of (a) listed securities, (b) securities designated by a Cabinet Order as being comparable to listed securities, and (3) other publicly offered securities subject to Art 4(1). In addition, Art 24(2) requires companies to file such a 'Periodic Securities Report' for the financial year preceding the date any securities issued by the companies are listed.

Article 24-5(1) provides that additional 'Semi-Annual reports' must be filed with the MOF. Any company required to file 'periodic securities reports' must also, under Art 24-5(2), file a 'Current Report' promptly on making any public offering of new or outstanding securities in a foreign country.

The contents of all the above reports are stipulated by ministerial ordinance. All reports so filed are made available to the public at the MOF, the head and major branch offices of the issuers, the relevant Stock Exchanges and the Securities Dealers Association.

III. Ad hoc disclosure requirements are imposed on all listed and registered companies by the various Japanese Stock Exchanges and the Securities Dealers Association. Under a 'timely disclosure policy', the Stock Exchanges and Securities Dealers Association require prompt disclosure of significant information likely to affect investors. Failure to comply with these requirements may lead to suspension of dealing in an issuer's securities. These requirements also function as a safeguard against insider dealing.

IV. Regarding the disclosure of tender offers, Art 27-2 requires that a 'registration statement of tender offer' be filed with the MOF whenever an offer is made to 'many and unspecified persons' to purchase shares outside the securities market. Article 27-3 requires that copies of such registration statements be delivered to the issuing companies involved, and Art 27-3(2) stipulates that matters significant to the public interest or needed for the protection of investors should be published in daily newspapers.

V. Failure to comply with the above disclosure requirements may lead to criminal and civil liabilities. Articles 197 & 198 provide for criminal liability for any false report of significant matters (the penalties being imprisonment for up to three years or a fine of up to 3 million yen) and for any offer or sale of securities which have not been validly registered (the penalties being imprisonment for up to one year or a fine of up to a million yen).

Hiroshi Oda
R Geoffrey Grice

Regulation of insider trading in Japan

Hiroshi Oda

I. The development of the Securities and Exchange Law

The Japanese government enacted a new Law on Securities and Exchange immediately after the end of the Second World War. This Law had been influenced by the Federal Securities Act and the Law on the Stock Exchange of the United States. Although the Law was passed by the Diet after obtaining the approval of the Allied Forces, in 1947, the Allied Forces demanded a total amendment of this new Law. The Americans demanded, *inter alia*, that a body similar to the Securities Exchange Commission, an independent self-regulatory body, should be set up. Also in the view of the Allied Forces, the Law had delegated too many powers to ministerial ordinances. The Japanese government bowed to these demands, and almost completely revised the Law. This Law— the Securities and Exchange Law of 1948—remains in force.[1]

The amended Law provides that, (1) the public offering of new or outstanding securities with a total par value over five million yen does not take effect until 30 days after reporting it to the Securities Exchange Commission, (2) the issuer of the securities is required to file a securities report with the Commission, (3) dealers in securities are required to register with the Commission, (4) all dealers may become underwriters, but may not become trustees for corporate bonds. Banks and other financial institutions may not deal in securities, (5) the manipulation of prices of listed securities and unlawful stabilization are prohibited. In addition, the Allied Forces issued a memorandum which prohibited trading in futures, which was to have a long-term effect on the Japanese Securities and Exchange system.

Since then, the Law has undergone more than 20 amendments. In 1952, the Securities Exchange Commission was abolished, and its powers were mostly transferred to the Ministry of Finance. An Advisory Committee on Securities

---

[1] There are two authoritative books on Securities and Exchange Law in Japanese: K. Kanzaki, *Shouken Torihiki Hou* (Securities and Exchange Law) (revised edition, Tokyo, 1987) and I. Kawamoto and T. Suzuki, *Shouken Torihiki Hou* (Securities and Exchange Law) (revised edition, Tokyo, 1987).

and Exchange was set up as a consultative body. Furthermore, two major reforms should be mentioned here. First, in 1971, there was a reform concerning disclosure and regulation of tender offers. The scope of companies subject to continuous disclosure requirements was broadened. Semi-annual reports and current reports were introduced in addition to annual reports. Securities reports filed with the Minister of Finance must now be made available for public inspection (Art 25). At the same time, the range of persons who are liable should a report be untrue on essential points was extended to cover public accountants, accounting firms, as well as principal underwriters, etc.

In addition, a new chapter on tender offers was added to the Law. The disclosure of relevant information is now required for a tender offer, and its terms and methods are regulated by the Law. Cabinet and ministerial orders concerning these matters were enacted to supplement the Law.

There was another significant development in 1971. As part of the financial liberalization, the Law on Foreign Securities Companies was enacted that year.[2] There is an enforcement order attached to this Law and also a ministerial ordnance. This Law allows foreign securities firms to conduct business in Japan, subject to obtaining a license for each branch office from the Minister of Finance. The deposit of a performance bond is required for each branch.

Then in 1981, there was a further amendment to the Law. This amendment mainly concerned the segregation of banking and securities business based on Art 65 of the Securities and Exchange Law. This provision was inspired by the US Glass-Steagall Act of 1933. Banks and other financial institutions have been entirely banned from securities business. The Japanese government had long been heavily relying on government bonds. As a result, the government bond market had expanded considerably and banks demanded entry into the market. Consequently, the Banking Law was substantially revised in 1981 in order to authorize banks and other financial institutions to deal in public bonds. Accordingly, provisions concerning the licensing of banks and other financial institutions for engaging in securities business were introduced into the Securities and Exchange Law. At the same time, the prohibitions against securities companies being engaged in banking businesses were relaxed. Furthermore, in 1985, the futures trade in public bonds became possible for securities companies and licensed financial institutions.[3]

The latest amendment took place in May 1988. This time, the amendment concerned disclosure, insider trading, and the stock index futures trade.

In addition to the Securities and Exchange Law, there are also two more laws to be mentioned. One is the Securities Investment Trust Law of 1951 (amended most recently in 1967), and the Law on Securities Investment Consultant Firms which was enacted in 1986.[4]

---

[2] An English translation of the Securities and Exchange Law and this Law is included in Japan Securities Research Institute, ed, *Japanese Securities Laws* (Tokyo, 1987).
[3] See Yūichi Ezawa's article in the present volume. Also A. Viner, *Inside Japan's Financial Markets* (London, 1987) pp 22–27.
[4] Law No 198, 1951 and Law No 74, 1986.

II.   An outline of the Securities and Exchange Law

The Securities and Exchange Law lists eight types of securities which are to be regulated by this Law (Art 2). The list includes government bonds, local government bonds, secured or unsecured corporate debentures, share certificate or subscription warrants and beneficiary certificates. In addition, other securities or certificates designated by cabinet order are to be covered by this Law.

The Law regulates securities transactions in various ways. First, the Law requires registration or licensing on certain occasions. Thus, a securities company should be a company limited by shares and must obtain a license from the Minister of Finance (Art 28). The Minister is empowered to revoke the license or suspend it for up to six months (Art 35). This is different from the American system, where securities companies are merely required to register.

The public offering of new or outstanding securities, as well as the tender offer of public securities, needs to be preceded by filing of a registration statement with the Minister of Finance (Arts 4, s 1, 27-2, s 1).

Second, there is a requirement of disclosure of relevant information. The disclosure system covers both initial distribution and subsequent trading. This topic is discussed in Osamu Kurihara's article in this volume.

The issuing company bears strict liability for loss caused by an untrue registering report or prospectus at the issuing stage. The amount of compensation is determined by the Law. Persons liable for compensation include directors of the issuing company, the owner of the outstanding securities pertaining to the public offering concerned, the public accountant who certified the report and the securities firm which entered into a principal underwriting contract with the issuer (Art 21, s 1).

The third method which the Law employs is the control of dealing within and outside the market. For instance, the Law prohibits manipulation of the market by creating an appearance of active trading, spreading rumours or making false representations (Art 125, ss 1 & 2). The fixing or stabilization of share prices is only allowed under strict conditions (s 3). Stabilization is allowed in cases where it is employed in order to facilitate an offer to the public of securities. Details are provided in a ministerial ordinance.

III.   New regulations on insider trading

In March 1988, the government submitted a bill to amend the Securities and Exchange Law to the Diet—Japanese Parliament—in order to strengthen controls over insider trading. The Diet passed this bill in May. The Law is expected to take effect in early 1989. One of the focuses of the amendment is insider trading.

Previously, Japanese Securities and Exchange Law has been unable to cope effectively with insider trading. First of all, there was no provision explicitly prohibiting insider trading. The closest to such a provision was Art 58 of the Law, which prohibits any person from employing fraudulent devices, schemes, or artifices with respect to buying, selling or other transactions involving securities. Violations of this provision may entail imprisonment for up to three years, or a maximum fine of three million yen (Art 197, sub-s 3). Furthermore, Art 50 lists unlawful activities of securities companies and their directors and employees. Subsection 3 prohibits them from committing acts related to buying and selling as well as other transactions, which are prescribed by Ministerial Ordinance as being contrary to the protection of investors, detrimental to the fairness of transaction, or undermining the credibility of the securities industry. Article 50 is applied *mutatis mutandis* to directors and employees of financial institutions dealing with public bonds (Art 65-2, sub-s 3). However, there were no corresponding penalties for the violation of these provisions.

These provisions were far from being an effective device for controlling insider trading. Article 50 is applicable only to directors and employees of securities companies. Article 58 is vague, and it was not clear at first sight whether this provision had something to do with insider trading, although specialists of securities and exchange law agreed that insider trading is covered and punishable by this provision. Besides, civil liability does not follow for its violations.

Article 58 has its origin in the Securities Exchange Act, s 10-b and Rules 10-b (5) of the United States. Whereas in the United States, this provision of the Act is duly enforced, in Japan, there has never been a reported case where this provision was applied. It can be argued that this provision would also work in Japan if it is properly implemented. However, it should be noted that in the United States, court judgments and the decisions of the SEC have produced a body of precedent that has helped to clarify this somewhat vague provision. In contrast, the principle of *nulla crimen sine lege* is strictly applied in Japan, and it was thought to be difficult to sustain a prosecution on the basis of Art 58.

This is not to say that insider trading seldom happens in Japan. On the contrary, because of the absence of an explicit provision banning insider dealing, it is often pointed out that people fail to perceive insider trading as being unlawful and often engage in such practices. There have been cases where the price of shares has soared immediately before a company increases its capital or announces a new product. Insider dealing was suspected in a number of cases, but it was often difficult to prove it, and most cases ended up with a warning from the Stock Exchange to the company concerned.

The only provision of the Securities and Exchange Law which was recently invoked to deal with insider trading is Art 189 on short-swing trading. Article 189 provides for the recovery of unfair profits obtained by directors or major shareholders of a company by their using information available to them by reason of their positions. If such persons make a profit by purchasing shares within six months after the sale, or selling shares within the same period after the purchase, the company may require this person to surrender such profits to the company (Art 189, s 1).

This provision has been combined with Art 188 which made the disclosure of purchase of the company's shares by its board members compulsory. After this provision was deleted by the amendment in 1966, there was no effective means to uncover short-swing trading. This made the enforcement of Art 189 extremely difficult in practice. In fact, Japanese companies have been rather lax in controlling trading in their securities by their employees and board members.

In addition to the Securities and Exchange Law, a ministerial ordinance on Standards of Soundness for Securities Companies was enacted in 1965. It prohibits board members and employees of securities companies from dealing in securities on the basis of special information obtained by reason of their positions in the company. Violations of this prohibition may result in administrative sanctions. But this ordinance has not been enforced strictly enough.

The need for strengthening control over insider trading has been accepted in Japan for some time. This was accelerated by two external factors. First, due to the internationalization of stock markets, especially with the close links which have developed between stock markets of the United States, Europe, and Japan, it is now possible to take advantage of inside information by dealing in a stock market of another country. Therefore, a concerted international approach to prevent transnational insider trading became indispensable. Since the early 1980s, the United States has concluded agreements on the exchange of information concerning insider trading with Switzerland, Canada, UK, and Japan. On the initiative of the US SEC, the Japanese Ministry of Finance is co-operating with its counterparts in other countries, including the UK Department of Trade and Industry, to take co-ordinated action towards the strengthening of control over insider trading.[5]

Another incident occurred in 1987 which accelerated this move. A medium-sized chemical company, which was heavily involved in 'financial strategy'—ie the practice of an industrial company of investing surplus funds in order to bolster profits, fell into financial difficulties. This company lost 20 billion yen in the sharp fall of the Japanese bond market. One of the banks which held shares in this company sold its holdings one day before this company announced its losses. A large number of shares were sold on the day before the announcement. The Ministry of Finance and the Osaka Stock Exchange investigated the case. Both failed to prove the existence of insider trading, but the former found that the bank acted against the informal guidance of the Ministry issued to listed companies, and was 'morally responsible'.[6]

After this incident, the Ministry of Finance hastened to take action to control insider trading. A special sub-committee on unfair trading in securities was established within the Securities and Exchange Advisory Committee, which is a consultative body reporting to the Minister of Finance. Upon the report of this sub-committee, the Advisory Committee published a report on the methods of regulating insider dealing.[7] The report recommended (1) the development of a system to prevent insider dealing, including the establishment of 'Chinese walls' between different departments within securities companies and ensuring the timely disclosure of relevant information, (2) the expansion of the power of the Minister of Finance to demand reports from listed companies and conduct investigations, (3) the obligatory reporting of directors and major shareholders when they have traded in their company's share, (4) the strengthening of criminal sanctions for insider trading.

The Ministry of Finance, upon receiving this report, drafted a bill to amend the Securities and Exchange law and submitted it to the Diet in March 1988.

[5] *Japan Financial Times*, 15 March 1988.
[6] *Japan Financial Times*, 6 October 1987.
[7] *Japan Financial Times*, 24 February 1988 (evening).

In the draft, two provisions were especially relevant. First, Art 190-2 which was newly added covers insider trading carried out by people 'connected with a company'. Those who have come to know significant facts concerning the business of listed companies are not allowed to sell or purchase securities (including options) of such a company or trade in them for profit except after these facts have been made public (Art 190-2, s 1). Securities in this context include listed shares, convertible bonds, bonds with warrants and straight bonds.

The scope of information which is considered to be insider is defined in s 2 of Art 190. This includes:

(1) Decisions of the executive body of a company to do or not to do the following: issue shares, convertible bonds, or bonds with warrants, decrease capital, divide shares, distribute profits, merge, effect a total or partial transfer of business or accept the transfer of business, initiate dissolution of the company or market new products or technology.
(2) Facts such as: losses resulting from natural disaster or business, changes in major shareholdings, facts which serve as grounds for termination of the listing of shares.
(3) The emergence of a difference between the latest publicized forecast of the amount of sales, operating profits, or net profits on one hand, and an updated forecast or year-end balance sheet on the other hand.

In addition, there is a general clause in sub-s (4), which covers 'significant facts concerning the business, or the assets of the company, which considerably affects the decision-making of investors'. Also Art 193-3 which provides for insider trading in tender offers covers facts concerning a tender offer or its cancellation.

The new Art 190-2 defines persons who are prohibited from using insider information. First, there are insiders, such as board members or employees of the issuing company, major shareholders with more than 10% of the issued shares of the company who are entitled to inspect the books of account. If the insider is a juridical person, its board members and employees are considered to be insiders. Those who ceased to be related to a company, for example, due to resignation, are nevertheless regarded as insiders for one year.

Second, there are quasi-insiders. The draft lists two categories of them: (1) a person who has a power granted by law over the company, (2) a person who is a party to a contract with the company (Art 190-2, s 1). The first category is rather vague, but it is understood to cover members of Parliament who have a power of legislative investigation, as well as ministerial officials responsible for supervising the industry. The second category includes trading partners of the issuing company as well as underwriters, attorneys, and accountants.

Third, those persons who have learned of significant facts concerning business from the above-mentioned persons are not allowed to trade in listed shares of the company before these facts are made public (Art 190-3, s 3). Thus, friends or families of these persons, and even a news reporter may be held liable for insider trading.

Violations of Arts 190-2 and 190-3 entail criminal sanctions: a maximum of six months' imprisonment or a fine not more than 500 thousand yen (Art 200, sub-s 4).

Initially, the Ministry of Finance had intended to list insiders and quasi-insiders in a ministerial ordinance rather than providing them in the Law. The Ministry of Justice argued that they should be explicitly included in the Law in order to make it known to the public that insider trading is an unlawful act and their view prevailed. A ministerial ordinance which is expected to be enacted shortly will merely provide for details.

On the other hand, the amendment has failed to provide for civil liability for insider trading. It is agreed that a system of compensation should be introduced into the Law. In fact, most specialists of Securities and Exchange Law are of the view that those who have suffered loss from insider trading are entitled to claim compensation on the ground of Art 709 of the Civil Code, which is the general provision on tort liability. However, it is very difficult to prove the existence of fault, a causal relationship, and quantity of damages in such cases. The drafters of the amendment thought it was premature to introduce a provision on civil liability in the Law, since issues such as the standing to sue, the adjudicative procedures, etc need to be discussed.

Another significant provision in the amendment concerns short-swing trading. The amendment strengthened control over securities transaction by board members or major shareholders of a company. Board members and major shareholders are required to file a report with the Minister of Finance, when they have purchased or sold the company's listed shares, convertible bonds, warranted bonds, or straight bonds or options on these securities before the 15th day of the forthcoming month (Art 188). The report is filed via the securities company. This provision, which had existed until the amendment of 1966, was thus reintroduced. Article 189 s 1 which provides for the short-swing trading remained almost unchanged by this amendment, but ss 4–9 were added in order to make the implementation of this provision stricter. Thus, when the Minister of Finance considers that a board member or a major shareholder has made a profit in breach of s 1, he informs this person of this finding. The latter may file an objection with the Minister. If there is no such objection, the Minister sends a copy of the relevant documents to the company and informs it of the transaction in expectation that the company will demand the surrender of the profits.

Even before this latest amendment, the Law had empowered the Minister of Finance to demand reports or submission of materials from the Stock Exchange concerning the state of its business or assets and also to make on-the-spot inspections when needed and appropriate to do so in the public interest or for the protection of investors (Art 154). This power of the Minister of Finance was extended to the issuing company of listed shares by the proposed amendment. Non-compliance with this provision entails a maximum fine of 300,000 yen (Art 206).

In response to the report of the Advisory Committee on Securities and Exchange securities companies have worked out self-regulatory mechanisms for insider trading. Compliance departments have been strengthened. Board members and employees of securities companies who have obtained significant information on an issuing company must now report it to the compliance department and unless a permission is given, may not disclose it even within the company. The compliance department is to keep information on mergers, increases in capital and other undisclosed information separate from other departments. The company is not to trade, on its own account, in the securities of a company concerning which there is insider information.[8]

The Ministry of Finance is planning to amend the Ministerial Ordinance and make it possible to recommend securities companies to take appropriate action when their system of information management is deficient.

The latest amendment to the Securities and Exchange Law is indeed a step forward in that insider trading is now explicitly declared unlawful. Of course, things cannot be changed by a single piece of legislation. Much depends on implementation of these provisions and with the current limited resources, this is not an easy task. Unlike the SEC in the United States, the Ministry of Finance does not have sufficient number of staff for monitoring securities transactions: there are only 180 people including local officials. Neither has the Stock Exchange enough staff. This amendment is merely a start, and certainly there is still far to go.

[8] *Japan Financial Times*, 20 February 1988.

Tokyo Stock Exchange listings and private placements by non-Japanese companies

Shinichi Saito and Robert F Grondine
Partners
Tokyo Aoyama Law Office

I.   Introduction

In the period 1987–1988, the Tokyo capital markets have assumed increasing significance in global financial markets.

With the continuing appreciation of the yen against most other currencies and especially against the United States dollar, the total capitalization of the shares listed on the Tokyo Stock Exchange (hereafter referred to as TSE) has surpassed the capitalization of shares listed on the New York Stock Exchange. Foreign currency reserves continue to rise at an astonishing rate, due in some significant part to the concerted efforts of the Japanese Ministry of Finance and the Bank of Japan to support the United States dollar in world currency markets.

Since 19 October 1987, the Tokyo Stock Exchange has fully recouped all losses incurred on that date and has since April and May 1988 forged to new all-time record highs for the Tokyo market. No other capital market in the world can make such a claim for rapid recovery from the global upheavals which occurred on 19 October 1987.

In this environment companies from around the world are focusing increasing attention on how to gain access to the Tokyo capital markets. The Japanese government continues to liberalize access to the Japanese capital markets by increasing the methods available to foreign companies for tapping Japanese capital in Japan. Since late 1987 these new efforts have resulted in the creation of Japanese *Samurai* Commercial Paper as the latest innovation.[1]

However, due to the various restrictions in the Japanese domestic capital markets generally, which will require further years to deregulate, many of these newer innovations have yet to develop fully. A particular problem continues to be the basic lack of depth and liquidity of secondary markets.

As a result of these considerations, two of the most favored means of gaining access to the Japanese capital markets at this date are listing on the Tokyo Stock

[1] As for Japanese securities market in general, see Yamashita & Grace, *Japan's Securities Market— A World Financial Centre* (Singapore, 1988).

Exchange and the placement of securities, either equity shares or other equity-type rights and/or debt instruments in the Japanese market through private placements. The first approach, listing on the Tokyo Stock Exchange, entails a high degree of regulation and cost, which are similar to the requirements for public listing of shares in many other countries. The second approach entails smaller unregulated offerings to Japanese investors, thereby taking advantage of Japanese capital markets without having to undergo the level of regulation and cost of a public offering of shares.

II.   Listing on the Tokyo Stock Exchange

In the fall of 1985, the number of non-Japanese companies listed on the Tokyo Stock Exchange was eight. The number reached approximately 90 by the end of 1987.[2] Some predictions indicate that this number could rise to 200 by 1989. As a result of these changes, an enormous amount of interest has been generated outside Japan in the rules and regulations which govern this listing process. The following section provides a brief introduction to the rules and regulations applicable to non-Japanese companies wishing to list their shares on the Tokyo Stock Exchange, as well as to general securities industry practices in Japan.[3]

1. TIME REQUIRED

Assuming that there is no substantial question as to the relevant company being able to satisfy the listing standards, it usually requires approximately three months from the submission of the application for listing until the completion of the listing. This three month period consists of two months for the review of the application documents by the Tokyo Stock Exchange and one month for review by the Ministry of Finance (hereafter referred to as MOF). The listing will take effect on the fourth business day after the final grant of the MOF approval for the listing.

If the applicant company does not have more than the required 1,000 shareholders in Japan (see below), the company is required in this interim period before listing to distribute shares in Japan so that the number of Japanese shareholders will be more than 1,000 as at the date of listing. If this is accomplished through a public offering and sale of the foreign company's securities in Japan, then before the company makes such a public offering and sale it must submit a securities registration statement to the MOF. It usually takes four to six weeks to obtain a response from the MOF as to whether the issuer may go ahead with such a public offering and sale.

---

[2] See Appendix III in A. Viner, *Inside Japan's Financial Markets* (London & Tokyo, 1987) pp 237–238.
[3] The information is primarily based upon the *Kabushiki Joujou Kijun* (Criteria for Listing of Shares) of the TSE. An English summary is available: TSE, *A Listing Guide for Foreign Companies* (Tokyo, 1986).

The period required for the public issue or other distribution of shares can be included in the above mentioned three month period, since such sales can take place during the review of the listing application by the TSE. The TSE review and the MOF's examination of the registration statement for the listing would proceed even during such public distribution of shares, based on an assurance by the Japanese securities company managing the listing that the required number of Japanese shareholders will be in place prior to the listing date.

In addition to the above minimum time requirement, two to four months will generally be necessary to prepare all documents (including all certified translations) for the securities registration statement and application for listing.

Accordingly, it usually requires a minimum of about six to eight months to list the stock of a foreign company from the decision by the company to proceed with the listing process until the completion of the listing.

However, the fiscal year end of the listing applicant must not fall between the time of the application's submission and the time of the listing. This rule stems from the idea that the application for listing must be based on the latest financial information for the applicant company publicly available at the time of the initial listing. The MOF and TSE will refuse to process an application if it is expected that the applicant's financial statements for a newly completed fiscal year will be published during the two month review application review process. In most cases, the listing will become effective in the five to eight months after the completion of the applicant's most recent fiscal year. Thus, it is recommended that the applicant start preparing application documents as soon as the financial information for the latest fiscal year has become available.

From the above considerations it should be obvious that a listing on the Tokyo Stock Exchange is a time-consuming process. The effort and expense required means that a high level commitment must be made by a foreign company before attempting a Tokyo Stock Exchange listing.

2. COSTS

Costs which will be incurred in the process of listing on the TSE always need to be estimated in yen terms, since all the costs will arise in yen. The following (estimated as at May 1988) is a list of relevant costs which will have to be incurred:

Listing examination fee	¥ 1,000,000
Listing fee (a + b) a. fixed	2,500,000
b. variable	(0.0045 yen per share)
Legal and CPA fee (total)*	13,000,000
Printing cost*	3,000,000
Misc	3,000,000
Total	¥ 22,500,000**

*subject to variation
**variable fee (0.0045 yen per share) excluded.

The above costs are for the process of the initial listing only and do not include any 'after listing costs', such as the following:

(1)	Annual levy to the TSE	¥ 540,000 *
(2)	Annual costs relating to continuous disclosure	4,000,000
(3)	Shareholder services (to custodian bank)	4,000,000
	Total	¥ 8,540,000

*This amount varies depending on the number of shares but is not significant.

None of the above estimations includes the fee payable to the securities company as manager of the listing process. Further, as indicated above it may also be necessary to conduct a public offering of shares or other share distribution in Japan in conjunction with the TSE listing in order to achieve the required minimum of 1,000 Japanese shareholders. All of these costs will be in addition to the basic listing costs indicated above, and must be negotiated with the Japanese securities company selected to manage the listing. The final amount of this fee will vary depending upon a large number of factors.

3. LISTING CRITERIA

Many foreign companies have completed listing their stock on the TSE during the recent past. There are no extraordinary requirements in relation to the application for listing by a United Kingdom or other non-Japanese company.
The following are the general minimum criteria for listing on the TSE.

A. Total number of shares to be listed

The Tokyo Stock Exchange does not impose an absolute minimum number of shares which must be proposed for listing. A TSE listing entails listing for trading purposes in Tokyo all shares of the listing company already registered for trading on its home stock exchange. Accordingly, the number of shares being listed for trading on the TSE will naturally be quite high.
It will be necessary to determine a minimum number of shares as a trading unit. That determination is made as follows:

If the total number of shares to be listed is	*The stock is to be traded in units of*	
over 20 million shares	a. 1,000	shares
over 2 million shares	b. 100	shares
over 1 million shares	c. 50	shares
over 200 thousand shares	d. 10	shares

The trading unit may also determined by the average closing price or quotation of the stock on the home stock exchange (or organized over-the-counter market in the home country) of the listing company for the six month period ending two weeks prior to the date of application for listing. If the applicant's stock price on its home exchange is relatively stable, then this rule will be relaxed substantially as follows:

If the average closing price for such period is		*The trading unit is set at*	
a.	less than ¥3,000	1,000	shares
b.	¥3,000 or more but less than ¥6,000	100	shares
c.	¥6,000 or more but less than ¥20,000	50	shares
d.	over ¥20,000	10	shares

B.   Number of shareholders in Japan

The foreign company must have 1,000 or more shareholders in Japan by the time of the effective date of the application for listing.

This minimum requirement is uniformly enforced. If the foreign applicant for listing does not currently have the required number of Japanese shareholders, then it may either (i) complete a public issue in Japan prior to the listing date, or (ii) arrange with a Japanese securities company for distribution of a sufficient number of shares privately during the period for preparation of the application.

As indicated above, the completion of a public offering of shares in Japan will require the submission of an application for approval of the offering to the MOF, as well as preparing substantial offering prospectuses and other formal documentation. These processes take time and involve substantial cost.

The second alternative is more flexible and less expensive. Accordingly, it has been more widely used. Of course, the securities company managing the listing will prefer the public offering approach, since that will normally command higher fees.

This second alternative is generally accomplished by the securities company purchasing a block of the listing company's shares outside Japan. These shares will then be sold through the securities company's broad network of branch offices within Japan. While it would appear that any such wide distribution of shares within Japan should be treated as a secondary distribution subject to registration requirements similar to any other public offering, this practice has been treated to date as a private placement of the relevant securities not subject to the registration requirements. Japanese securities companies support this interpretation on the basis that no single branch office sells to investors in excess of the number which would result in characterization as a public offering. To our knowledge, their interpretation has not been challenged by the MOF.

C.   Trading in the home country, etc

The applicant's stock must have good liquidity in its home country or other principal market.

D.   Net assets (shareholder's equity)

The applicant must have total net assets equivalent to 10 billion yen or more as of the end of the business year prior to its application for listing.

E.   Profit

The applicant's profit before taxes in each of the past three fiscal years must have been the equivalent of at least two billion yen.

F.   Dividends

The applicant must have paid dividends in each of the three business years preceding the application for listing, and there must be a reasonable prospect that it will be able to continue paying dividends after listing.

G.   Time elapsed since incorporation

By the end of the last business year prior to its application for listing, the applicant must have been incorporated as a joint stock company and continuously in business for at least five years.

H.   Stock exchange on which the securities are listed

The applicant must be listed in its country of origin on a stock exchange recognized by the TSE.

I.   Form of stock certificates

The form of stock certificates issued by the listing applicant must conform with requirements established by the TSE. Since the applicant will already have complied with such requirements of its home exchange, and in light of the large number of major international corporations which have now been listed on the TSE, it appears that this requirement should not pose any substantial burden.

J.   Designation of shareholder service agent and dividend disbursing bank

The applicant must appoint in Japan a shareholder service agent and a bank to disburse dividends, or have obtained informal acceptance of such appointments, prior to the date of its application for listing.

K.   Corporate resolutions

Certain corporate resolutions approving the company's decision to list on the TSE are required by the TSE and MOF. Passage of these resolutions represents the first formal step in commencing the listing process.

L.   Power of attorney

A power of attorney is required for evidence of the authority of the various persons who will be executing documents in connection with the listing application.

M.   List of documents submitted in Japanese and required information

At least twenty kinds of documents must be submitted with the listing application, and their preparation is very time-consuming. Mostly, they will be prepared by the Japanese securities company, and the accounting and law firms retained by the applicant company.

(1)   DOCUMENTS

The main documents required in a listing application are as follows:

1. Securities report for the application for listing, Volume I.

2. Securities report for the application for listing, Volume II.

3. Application for new listing of securities.

4. Stock listing agreement.

5. Legal opinion by General Counsel of applicant.

6. Written acceptance of the appointment from the stockholder service agent.

7. Written acceptance of the appointment from the bank responsible for disbursing dividends.

8. Certificate of Incorporation and By-Laws with certificate by secretary (constitutive documents).

9. Document certifying the resolution of the board of directors as to the application for listing.

10. Document certifying that the person acting as representative of Applicant is duly authorized.

11. Specimen certificate(s) of stock of applicant with cover letter.

12. Document certifying that the stock of Applicant is listed on home country securities exchange.

13. Description of the shareholders in Japan.

14. Description of the trading of Applicant stock on its home exchange and other exchanges where listed.

15. Description of changes in the price of Applicant's stock on its home exchange and other exchanges where listed.

16. Letter of recommendation by a securities company (ie the Japanese securities company managing the listing) to the TSE.

17. Memorandum (prescribed).

18. Power of attorney authorizing legal counsel.

19. Forms 10-K (US) (or other country's equivalent) for the last three years.

20. Forms 10-Q (US) (or other country's equivalent) for the last three years.

21. Reports submitted to SEC (or other local regulatory authority) for the last three years.

22. Annual reports for the last five years.

23. Quarterly Reports for the last three years (or three and a half years if the latest semi-annual issue is available).

24. Materials released to press for the last three years.

(2) MAJOR INFORMATION REQUIRED

The types of information required to be produced with an application for a TSE listing are presented in three parts: the formal Application for Listing, the Securities Report Volume I, and the Securities Report Volume II.

a. The application for listing of stock

The Application for Listing of Securities is a set of documents to be submitted by the applicant to the President of the Exchange. It must carry the name and seal (or signature) of the authorized representative of the company applying for listing. The major items of information to be furnished in the Application are:

1. Description of the stock for which application is being made (ie, name of the issue; registered/bearer form; class; par value/non-par value; amount of par value, if applicable; and the amount of such stock outstanding).
    If there are any unissued shares which the applicant has resolved to issue before the application date, or if any additional shares beyond the number for which application is being made are expected to be issued as a result of the exercise of a conversion privilege or 'equity elements' of the company's other securities, then the number of such authorized but unissued shares must also be furnished.
2. Other securities issued by the company.
3. Detailed information on the number of shares outstanding and the amount of capital.

4. Purposes of the company.
5. Outline of the company's business.
6. Terms and conditions of any public offering or secondary distribution conducted during the three-year period preceding the listing application date.
7. Number of shares held by directors.
8. Number of shares held by principal stockholders.
9. Distribution of ownership of shares (by type of holder, size of holding, and geographical distribution in Japan).

b.   The Securities Report (Volume I)

Volume I of the Securities Report is to be prepared in accordance with Form 7 (information to be furnished in the Securities Registration Statement) as prescribed by ministerial ordinance promulgated under the Securities and Exchange Law (hereafter referred to as SEL).[4] This volume of the Report will be available for public inspection and is divided into two parts.

PART I

1. Outline of Legal and Other Systems in the Country of Origin: (1) outline of corporate system; (2) foreign exchange control system; (3) tax treatment; (4) transactions for market stabilization; and (5) legal opinions.

2. Outline of the Company: (1) history of the company; (2) amount of paid-in capital; (3) changes in paid-in capital; (4) total number of shares; (5) distribution of shares by type of stockholder; (6) trends in per-share dividends, etc; (7) trends in market price and trading volume; (8) description of parent company and subsidiaries; (9) directors and officers; and (10) employees.

3. Outline of Business: (1) purposes of the company and nature of business; and (2) material contracts.

4. Outline of Business Operations: (1) general; (2) production capacity; (3) production records; (4) orders booked and production plans; and (5) sales results.

5. Condition of Facilities: (1) facilities; (2) new facilities installed, significant expansions or improvements of existing facilities, and plans for such installation, expansion or improvement; and (3) disposal, renewal or loss of fixed assets.

6. Financial Condition: (1) financial statements (all of which must be accompanied by an audit report); (2) major assets and liabilities, and revenues and expenditures; and (3) cash flow. Until several years ago, the TSE required that all financial statements submitted for these purposes had to be translated to Japanese generally accepted auditing practices, both initially and on an ongoing basis. That requirement placed a heavy cost burden on foreign

---

[4] An English translation of the Securities and Exchange Law is published as Japan Securities Research Institute , ed, *Japanese Securities Laws and Relating Orders* (Tokyo, 1987).

companies wishing to list in Tokyo, and was cited as one central reason for the decline in the number of foreign companies listed on the TSE from 1978 through 1985. In order to remove that barrier, the requirement of dual auditing and Japanese Government Accepted Accounting Principles financial statements was eliminated.

7. Outline of Agreements on Share-handling Services, etc, in Japan.

PART II

Latest Financial Statements: financial statements for each of the past five business years (or, for companies whose accounting period is six months, the past ten business terms) excluding any information already contained in PART I above.

c. *The Securities Report (Volume II)*

The items of information to be furnished in this Volume II of the Securities Report are stipulated in the Exchange's listing regulations. Information already furnished in Volume I need not be repeated in Volume II. If there are difficulties in preparing this volume because of differences in the corporate disclosure systems in the home market and Japan or for other specific reasons, this volume may be prepared in such other form as the TSE deems appropriate in each case. This volume of the Report will not be available for public inspection.

1. Reasons for Applying for Listing.

2. Outline of Disclosure System in the Home Market and Related Matters.

3. History of the Company: (1) changes of substance in the applicant's business; and (2) details of business performance, capital structure, etc, for each business term ended within the last ten years.

4. Shareholdings of Directors, Officers, and Principal Shareholders: number of shares held by each director or officer, and changes in principal shareholders during the last five years.

5. Stock Options and Other Rights.

6. Personnel Administration and condition of Facilities: (1) outline of managerial and organizational structure; (2) wages and salaries of employees; and (3) facilities installed, sold or removed during the last five years.

7. Characteristics of the company, Products, etc, and Competitive Position.

8. Outline of Business: (1) purchases of materials and/or merchandise; and (2) sales.

9. Financial Condition: corporate accounting system in the home market.

10. Companies related to the Applicant by Virtue of Personnel or Capital.

11. Present Situation and Future Outlook: (1) dividend policy; and (2) plans for acquisition of capital and plans with respect to facilities.

Most of the above information will be obtained by the documentation team through, in the case of companies listed on US stock exchanges (whether or not they are US corporations), Forms 10-K, 10-Q and annual reports filed in the United States, and in all other cases from the equivalent disclosure documents filed with the stock exchange and regulatory authorities in the foreign company's home country or other listing jurisdiction(s). Therefore, the company applying for listing need not try to gather substantial additional information until any specific needs are identified in the documentation process.

III.   Private placements in the Japanese market

Securities issued by a foreign company either within or outside Japan fall within the definition of Japanese securities under Japanese law. The solicitation of persons to purchase securities is generally regulated under the SEL.

The purchase of shares and other equity-type rights as well as debt instruments issued by a foreign corporation and the remittance of funds abroad in respect of such purchases is generally regulated under the Foreign Exchange and Foreign Trade Control Law (hereafter FEFTCL).

1. REGULATIONS UNDER THE SECURITIES AND EXCHANGE LAW (SEL)

Under SEL Art 2 s 1, shares in a foreign corporation and debt instruments issued by a foreign corporation are specifically included within the definition of 'securities'. A public offering or secondary distribution of securities gives rise to an obligation to register such public offering or secondary distribution by submitting a registration statement to the Ministry of Finance (SEL Art 4). In addition, a prospectus in relation to the public offering or secondary distribution must also be prepared (SEL Art 13).

However, a public offering and a secondary distribution are defined under the SEL as offers to many and unspecified persons. Offers of securities to a few specified individuals do not fall within such definition and are not covered by the registration requirement.

According to a circular issued by the Ministry of Finance, offers of securities to 'many unspecified individuals' means 50 or more persons. Consequently, an offering of shares to 49 or fewer investors will not constitute a public offering or secondary distribution under the SEL and will be treated as a 'private placement' not subject to the SEL registration requirement.

Although a prospectus is also not expressly required, it has become standard practice in Japanese private placements to prepare and distribute to investors some form of offering circular or placement memorandum. Generally, such documents are fairly simple, containing basic descriptions of the company's business situation and financial and corporate structure.

Normally the placement memorandum will be prepared by the securities company acting as manager or arranger for the issue of securities. Though use of a securities company is not required for a private placement of securities, preparation by the issuer of a placement memorandum is nevertheless recommended.

No specific disclaimers are expressly required as to the fact that the offering of the securities has not been registered, reviewed or approved by any particular regulatory authority within Japan. However, the usual practice of securities companies when arranging a private placement is to include certain confirmations from the issuer and related disclaimers in the placement memorandum. As compared with the detailed list of warnings and disclaimers found in private placement memoranda in the United States, and to a lesser extent in other countries, the Japanese approach will appear to be highly anaemic. Accordingly, foreign offerors may feel unprotected in respect of claims by Japanese investors after an investment has gone sour.

Furthermore, Japan does not have any rule similar in scope or effectiveness to the United States anti-security fraud provision embodied in Rule 10b-5. Nor do the Japanese securities laws purport to provide private causes of action to investors for failure to comply with all the technical regulatory requirements established under the SEL.[5]

In essence, therefore, Japanese investors are left to pursue claims in such cases based upon general fraud provisions and gross negligence provisions in the Japanese Civil and Commercial Codes. As in any country, proof of fraud in Japan requires demonstration of actual intent to defraud and represents one of the most difficult cases to prove in litigation. This is especially so in Japan which has no effective discovery procedures to investigate the other party to a litigation through court-enforced sanctions.

Liability for gross negligence requires proof of a definitive safety or disclosure standard applicable to the defendant. Since Japanese securities laws impose only very minimal disclosure standards, if these are met then there should exist no additional basis for negligence liability.

As a result of these considerations, the possibility of litigation in Japan in respect of claims by a Japanese investor against a foreign issuer is quite minimal. Historically there have been very few cases of litigation commenced in Japan in respect of securities investments. Nonetheless, a foreign party seeking to make a private placement in Japan should strive to include in the private placement memorandum as many warnings and disclaimers as can realistically be included at the time of offering. Provided a reasonable warning to the investors has been included, then it should not be possible for a disappointed investor to succeed against an issuer by claiming fraud or gross negligence.

2. OUTLINE OF REGULATION UNDER THE FOREIGN EXCHANGE AND FOREIGN TRADE CONTROL LAW AND RELATED PROCEDURES THEREUNDER

The acquisition of foreign securities by a Japanese resident from a non-resident

---

[5] However, see Professor Oda's article in this volume for the new regulations on insider trading.

is one of the enumerated 'capital transactions' under FEFTCL Art 20(sub-s 5). In certain situations, such acquisition will be further designated as a 'direct foreign investment' under FEFTCL Art 22(s 2).[6]

(i) Treatment as a capital transaction

Generally, a Japanese resident effecting a capital transaction involving the purchase of foreign securities (for at least the equivalent of 10 million yen) must submit a notification to the Minister of Finance, through the Bank of Japan, no earlier than ten days prior to such acquisition (Ministerial Ordinance Concerning Foreign Exchange Control, Art 9). The investor may then effect the transaction immediately after filing the prior notification (FEFTCL) Art 23(1)). However, since there is a chance that receipt of the notification could be refused by the MOF or the Bank of Japan for improper preparation of documents, etc, it is advisable to submit the notification at least one week prior to the intended date of acquisition of the securities.

   The actual procedures required to be taken by investors are filing in triplicate the notification of capital transaction. No other regulatory requirements would apply to such purchases by Japanese investors. Foreign issuers would not be subject to any obligations for filing under the FEFTCL.

(ii) Treatment as a direct foreign investment

A 'direct foreign investment' is a type of capital transaction and is defined as the acquisition of any securities issued by a foreign juridical person, or lending any money to a foreign juridical person, designated by Cabinet Order as an act purporting to establish a long-term economic relationship therewith, or any payment of funds for establishment or expansion of a branch, factory or other place of business in a foreign country by a Japanese resident (FEFTCL Art 22, s 3). The relevant Cabinet Order prescribes the criteria under which an acquisition of foreign securities will be classified as a direct foreign investment as follows:

1. the Japanese investor acquires 10% or more of total value of foreign securities issued by the relevant foreign issuing corporation;
2. the Japanese investor already holds 10% interest in a foreign company and acquires an additional interest therein by a further acquisition of securities; and
3. in connection with an acquisition of foreign securities, the Japanese investor maintains with the foreign company a long-term relationship of the kind designated by Ministerial Ordinance, such as holding a directorship position, having a long-term supply agreement for raw materials or important production technology, etc.

---

[6] An English translation of the FEFTCL and related ordinances is published as *Japan: Laws, Ordinances, and other Regulations concerning Foreign Exchange and Foreign Trade* (Tokyo, 1987).

If any of the above criteria are met, the acquisition of foreign securities will be considered a direct foreign investment, in which case the investor must file a notification with the Minister of Finance through the Bank of Japan no earlier than two months prior to the proposed acquisition. The Minister of Finance has 20 days to review the notification and during such period may recommend that the acquisition be modified or suspended. Provided the.Minister does not make a recommendation within this period, the investor may acquire the foreign securities after 20 days have elapsed from the filing of the notification. The Minister of Finance also has the discretion to shorten this waiting period.

Under relevant administrative guidance practices of the Ministry of Finance, when the value of a direct foreign investment is the equivalent of 20 million dollars or more, the Japanese investor must also submit (in addition to the standard notification) a report on the 'outline of operations of the object of investment'. This report is first examined by the Ministry or Finance. If approved, the notification of direct foreign investment will be accepted by the Bank of Japan. If the Ministry of Finance does not approve of the investment, the Bank of Japan will not accept the notification.

(iii) Procedures after acquisition of shares

Where the acquisition of shares is treated simply as a capital transaction, the investor is not required to make any notifications after acquiring the shares. Consequently, no reporting obligation is imposed on the investor at the time of actual remittance of funds or upon the transfer of such shares to a third party. However, in certain cases the Bank of Japan may require the filing of post-acquisition reports.

Where the acquisition of shares is treated as a direct foreign investment, normally no post-acquisition report is required. However, submission of a 'Report concerning direct foreign investment' to the Minister of Finance through the Bank of Japan is required in the following cases:

a. subsequent disposal of shares (including preferential redemption upon capital reduction);
b. suspension of operation of entire notified transaction;
c. dissolution of the foreign corporation.

In the case of all of these requirements under the FEFTCL, for the most part they will involve only ministerial notifications which will not pose any substantial barrier to the investor completing the intended purchase of securities issued by a foreign corporation. There continue to exist, however, restrictions on Japanese companies investing in certain types of foreign businesses. If the foreign issuer of the relevant securities is engaged in one of those businesses and the relevant purchase will constitute a 'foreign direct investment', then the MOF or the Bank of Japan may refuse the notification or impose significant delays or other administrative requirements.

Generally the areas of most concern in this regard are companies engaging in the following businesses: arms manufacturing, fisheries and agriculture, leather and leather goods, petroleum. In addition, the MOF on occasion has raised some barriers in respect of investment in foreign financial institutions by

Japanese corporations which are not engaged in a financial business in Japan. Also, during the period immediately following the Plaza Accord in September 1985, the MOF engaged in a concerted effort to slow the flow of capital out of Japan temporarily so as to influence the change in the Yen-US dollar exchange rate. The same concern can arise from time to time, resulting in some administrative delays in completing the required notifications but not any ultimate prohibition of the intended transaction.

In summary, while the existence of the FEFTCL requirements does impose some timing limitations and administrative cost on the process of completing private placements in the Japanese market, generally these will be only minor considerations in the overall context of the private placement transaction. However, since violation of these requirements can result in criminal penalties and civil and administrative fines in egregious cases, they should be carefully considered and fulfilled in all cases.

IV. Conclusion

As can be seen from the discussion, the technical aspects of listing on the TSE and private placements in the Japanese market can be quite complicated and deserve considerable attention before making any commitment to entering the Japanese capital markets via either of these routes. Compared to the legal and administrative red tape required to access the capital markets in the United States, however, the Japanese requirements must be considered quite reasonable and bearable. Compared to access to the Euromarkets, however, these Japanese requirements may be somewhat harsh. The costs, both current and continuing, of choosing the Japanese market should be compared carefully with other available markets before embarking upon this considerable undertaking.

In the long term, however, given the ever growing importance of the Japanese capital markets and Japanese institutional investors in the world financial markets, most major multinational companies will over the next decade be faced with an increasing need to tap capital sources in Japan. Under these circumstances it behoves all players in the world financial markets to become more familiar with the workings and parameters of the Japanese capital markets.

Appendix I

TIMETABLE FOR INITIAL LISTING

The timetable given below is a guide to the time required for listing stock on the Exchange for the first time. The formal application for listing may be made only after the applicant's board of directors resolves to list on the Exchange and the listing application and supporting documents are completed.

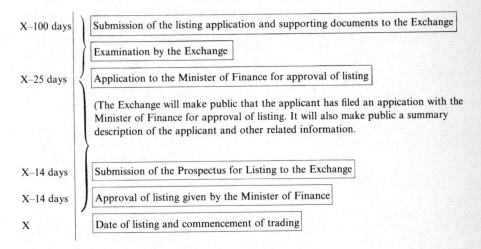

X–100 days — Submission of the listing application and supporting documents to the Exchange

Examination by the Exchange

X–25 days — Application to the Minister of Finance for approval of listing

(The Exchange will make public that the applicant has filed an appication with the Minister of Finance for approval of listing. It will also make public a summary description of the applicant and other related information.

X–14 days — Submission of the Prospectus for Listing to the Exchange

X–14 days — Approval of listing given by the Minister of Finance

X — Date of listing and commencement of trading

Note: If a public offering of new or outstanding stock under the Securities and Exchange Law is contemplated in conjunction with listing for the purpose of creating the required minimum number of shareholders in Japan, procedures for the public offering may extend the above timetable by about one month.

TSE: *A Listing Guide for Foreign Companies* (Tokyo, 1986) p 12.

Appendix II

DISCLOSURE OF MATERIAL INFORMATION AFTER LISTING

A foreign company whose stock is listed on the Exchange is expected to disclose material information in a satisfactory manner so as to ensure the protection of Japanese investors. Disclosure after listing is made through a proxy resident in Japan representing the listed foreign company, as shown in the following chart:

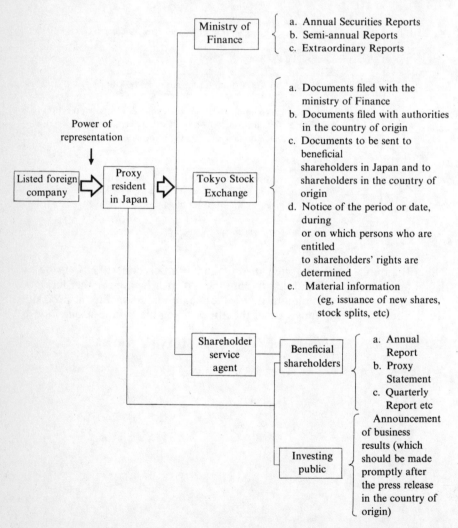

Note : In principle, all documents exceed those filed with authorities in the country of origin must be in Japanese.

TSE: *A Listing Guide for Foreign Companies* (Tokyo, 1986) p 14.

III.   Anti-Monopoly Law

An outline of the Japanese Anti-Monopoly Law

Hiroshi Oda

INTRODUCTION

The industrialization of Japan, which started in the late nineteenth century, was initiated and promoted by the government from above, rather than by the spontaneous growth of the entrepreneurs from below. At the initial stage, the government promoted and managed key industries and then handed them over to private companies at an extremely low price. This resulted in a domination of the economy by a handful of giant business conglomerates which were called *zai-batsu*.[1]

Furthermore, in the 1930s, new laws were enacted in order to facilitate the military build-up. This led to a further concentration of economic power. Thus the concentration of economic power was not necessarily regarded as a negative phenomenon in Japan.

One of the goals which the Allied Forces endeavoured to achieve after the Second World War was the democratization of the economy. This included the dissolution of *zai-batsu*, and elimination of the excessive concentration of economic power. It was against this background that the Law on the Prohibition of Private Monopoly and the Maintenance of Fair Trade (hereafter Anti-Monopoly Law) was enacted.[2] In the same year, the Fair Trade Commission was established in order to implement this law. The commission is organizationally attached to the Prime Minister's Office, but is guaranteed independence and has quasi-judicial and legislative powers.

The Anti-Monopoly Law, which was introduced in 1947, was heavily influenced by the anti-trust legislation of the United States. It was even stricter than the American law in some aspects, since American advisers to Japan were inclined to support the precepts of the New Deal policy, and intended to introduce a system which they had failed to implement fully in the United States. However, this legislation was considered to be too stringent to be applied to Japan—a country which had previously rejected any idea of regulating the concentration of economic power and promoting fair competition. Therefore,

[1] R. Storry, *A History of Modern Japan* (Harmondsworth, 1960) pp 123–124.
[2] Law No 54, 1947.

the restrictions introduced by the Anti-Monopoly Law were relaxed by an amendment in 1953, soon after the end of the Allied occupation.

Another major reform of the Anti-Monopoly Law took place in 1977. This was the time when there was considerable public criticism of the behaviour of major corporations during the oil crisis, and, for the first time in the history of the Anti-Monopoly Law, restrictions were strengthened. This amendment introduced, *inter alia*, (1) surcharges for operating illegal cartels, (2) the new concept of 'monopolistic situation' which enables the Fair Trade Commission to order the partition of giant companies, (3) the submission of reports to the Fair Trade Commission in cases of parallel price fixing.

The Anti-Monopoly Law is to promote and maintain free and fair competition in the market and to ensure fair trade. Article 1 of the Law provides that the Law is to promote free and fair competition, enhance free enterprise, encourage business activity, and increase employment and wage levels. This provision is interpreted broadly to include not only fairness of competition, but also fairness of trade. This Law is expected to contribute to the protection of the interests of consumers and ultimately, to the democratic development of the nation's economy. In order to achieve these purposes, the Law prohibits private monopolization, unreasonable restraints on trade, and unfair trade practices. Furthermore, it provides for measures to prevent the excessive concentration of economic power and to eliminate undue restraints over production, sales, technology, etc.

The agency in charge of implementing the Anti-Monopoly Law is the Fair Trade Commission. Organizationwise, the Fair Trade Commission is attached to the Prime Minister's office (Art 27). The chairman and four councillors of the Fair Trade Commission are appointed by the Prime Minister with the consent of both Houses. The appointment of the chairman is sanctioned by the Emperor. The chairman and the councillors are required to be over 35, and have sufficient knowledge of either economics or law. Once they are appointed they may not be removed against their will, except in cases specified by the Law (Art 31).

The Anti-Monopoly Law of Japan regulates the activities of *entrepreneurs*. The Law defines an entrepreneur as a person who carries on commercial, industrial, or financial business (Art 2, s 1). Entrepreneurs can be either natural persons or juridical persons. Local authorities, as well as government agencies, may also qualify. The Law further provides for *trade associations*. A trade association is defined as a union of entrepreneurs or a federation of such unions, which has the promotion of their common entrepreneurial interests as its primary goal.

The sanctions provided by the Anti-Monopoly Law can be applied to those entrepreneurs or trade associations which, in one way or another, restrict fair competition within a 'particular field of trade'. Whether foreign markets are included in this definition is not certain. Generally, it is understood that restrictions on fair competition in a foreign market cannot be controlled by the Japanese Anti-Monopoly Law, unless it directly affects the domestic market.[3]

The Anti-Monopoly Law covers three major areas: private monopolization, unreasonable restrictions on trade, and unfair methods of trading.

[3] M. Matsushita, *Keizaihou Gairon* (An Outline of Economic Law) (Tokyo, 1986) p 49.

I.   Prohibition of private monopolization and other forms of concentration of economic powers

1. PRIVATE MONOPOLIZATION

Article 3 of the Anti-Monopoly Law prohibits entrepreneurs from operating private monopolization. The term 'private monopolization' means the exclusion or control of business activities of other entrepreneurs, thus substantially reducing competition, such as to be against public interest (Art 2, s 5). This includes prohibition of private monopolization itself, as well as control of excessive concentration of economic power and control of 'monopolistic situation'.

Typical acts of excluding other entrepreneurs are: unreasonable reductions in price, predatory pricing and the acquisition of competing entrepreneurs. Control of other entrepreneurs' activity means depriving an entrepreneur of his freedom of decision-making. Typical cases include holding the shares of a competitor and abuse of bargaining power.

There was a case where a tin-manufacturing company exercised control over four smaller companies by holding their shares through intermediaries and sending in directors to these companies. In order to maintain its dominant position, the company, *inter alia*, restricted the business of these smaller companies by limiting the size of the market to which they sold the goods, prohibiting the manufacturing of certain goods and obstructing the construction of a new plant. When a food company planned to open its own plant for manufacturing tin, the company stopped supplying its products to the tin-manufacturing company and forced the former to abandon the project. As a result, this company managed to gain a 74% market share. The Fair Trade Commission found this to be private monopolization.[4]

Private monopolization can be realised not only by the actions of a single entrepreneur, but also through a concerted action of entrepreneurs. In one case, two dairy companies (at one time a single company which had been split up after the Second World War), collected more than 70% of milk supplies in a region. They colluded with the Agricultural Bank and the regional Federation of Agricultural Co-operatives. The companies were able to exercise influence over them because they were shareholders and directors of the companies were also on the boards of the Bank and Federation. The Bank made it a condition of loans to dairy suppliers (farmers) that the latter would not supply milk to competitors of the two dairy companies. The Federation imposed a similar condition for guaranteeing such loans. For over three years, the Bank extended 300 million yen in loans and was able to affect severely the business of its competitors. Thus, the dairy companies managed to maintain its dominant position and even to strengthen it by restricting or eliminating the business of its competitors. The Fair Trade Commission found this to be private monopolization.[5]

---

[4] Recommendatory Decision of the Fair Trade Commission, 18 September 1972 (FTC *Shinketsushū* 19-87: Touyou Seikan case).
[5] Decision of the Fair Trade Commission, 28 July 1956 (FTC *Shinketsushū* 8-12: Yukijirushi Dairy case).

In another case, a leading producer of soy sauce which had a market share of 9.3% decided to raise the price of its products. The company stopped supplying those retail traders who did not increase their prices. In this field of business, the price was considered to reflect the quality of the product, and as a result of this company's act, other major companies were forced to raise the price as well. The Fair Trade Commission found that by controlling the resale price of the product, this company had restrained fair competition.[6]

The Fair Trade Commission is entitled to order an entrepreneur to file reports with the Commission, to cease certain acts, to transfer part of the business and take other necessary measures to eliminate any abuses. Thus, in the above-cited dairy companies case, the Fair Trade Commission recommended this company to stop interfering in other companies' activities and sell those shares which the company owned through intermediaries.

2. CONTROL OF EXCESSIVE CONCENTRATION OF ECONOMIC POWER

The Anti-Monopoly Law restricts the holding of shares, the concurrent holding of directorships, the merger of companies and the transfer of business. These restrictions are aimed at preventing the concentration of economic power in the hands of a small number of entrepreneurs.

There is a general prohibition on creating a share-holding company (Art 9). Share-holding company means a company, the primary business of which is to control the business activities of another company in Japan by holding its shares. Before the Second World War, *zai-batsu* had controlled groups of companies through such holding companies. This provision was introduced to prevent the re-emergence of such *zai-batsu*. The provision, however, does not prohibit companies from holding shares if they are, at the same time, engaged in business. Therefore, it is possible to establish a subsidiary and hold its shares as long as the parent company itself is engaged in some kind of business.

The acquisition and holding of other companies' shares is restricted by law. First, companies are forbidden to acquire or hold shares of a company, if this results in substantially limiting competition in a particular field. They are also banned from acquiring or holding shares by unfair means of trade (Art 10, s 1). The Fair Trade Commission issued guidelines in 1981 for the application of this provision.[7]

There are special restrictions dealing with financial companies. Banks, securities companies and insurance companies may not acquire or hold more than 5% of the issued shares of another company in Japan (Art 11).

Another restriction on the owning of shares by companies was introduced by the 1977 amendment. Large companies limited by shares whose net assets exceed 30 billion yen or which have capital of more than 10 billion yen, are now prohibited from acquiring or holding shares beyond a certain limit. The ceiling is set at the amount of net assets or capital, whichever is the higher. The total

---

[6] Judgment of the Tokyo Appellate Court, 25 December 1957 (*Kousai Minshū* 10-12-743: Noda Shouyu case).
[7] M. Nakagawa, *Anti-Monopoly Legislation in Japan* (Tokyo, 1984) pp 89–94.

price of acquisition should not exceed this ceiling (Art 9-2, s 1). However, various exceptions, such as companies which develop natural resources, are made to this provision.

The Law also has restrictions on mergers. A merger with a Japanese company is not allowed, if (1) as a result of the merger, competition in a particular field is likely to be substantially limited, or, (2) unfair trade practices have been employed in the course of the merger (Art 15, s 1). A company which intends to merge with another company must file a report with the Fair Trade Commission (ibid, s 2). The merger cannot be carried out until 30 days after the report has been received by the Commission (ibid, s 3). The Commission is to decide whether the merger is likely to limit competition substantially within this period. If the conclusion is in the affirmative, it will recommend that the parties refrain from merging or initiate formal proceedings. If the Commission finds that the merger is against the Law, it may prohibit the merger or impose conditions on merger. When the merger is carried out in breach of the Law, the Commission is empowered to bring the case to court and nullify the merger (Art 18).

The only case of merger which the Fair Trade Commission has formally handled is the merger of Fuji Steel Corporation and Yawata Steel Corporation. In the mid 1960s, the Japanese steel industry was dominated by six major companies. The first and the second largest companies decided to merge and filed a report with the Fair Trade Commission in accordance with the Law. The Commission found the merger to be unlawful, ie it was likely substantially to limit competition, and recommended that the merger not go ahead. This was not accepted by the two companies. Therefore, the Commission applied to the Tokyo Appellate Court for an injunction, which was granted. The Commission then initiated formal proceedings. Both companies, seeing that it was difficult to obtain approval for the merger, chose to accept the decision of the Commission. Accordingly, the Commission rendered a consentient decision.[8]

The Commission ruled that when, as a result of a merger, the structure of the market changes, becomes less competitive, and one entrepreneur obtains a dominant position within the market, it is a substantial restraint on competition such as within Art 15, s 1. An entrepreneur is considered to hold a dominant position, if this entrepreneur dominates the market, or is capable of controlling the price, quality or quantity of the merchandise to a certain extent. As regard this particular case, the Commission acknowledged, in principle, that the proposed merger would result in a substantial restriction of competition in the market of rails, tin plate and other items. However, the Commission ruled that if necessary measures to prevent unreasonable restraints were adopted, such restraints could be avoided and the merger could go ahead. Thus, various measures, such as the transfer of steel furnaces as well as expertise to other smaller companies and the sale of shares owned by the parties, were recommended and accepted by the two companies. The idea underlying this decision is that if an effective competitor is created, the proposed merger will not result in a substantial restraint on fair competition.

The Fair Trade Commission issued guidelines concerning mergers in 1980.

---

[8] Consentient Decision of the Fair Trade Commission, 30 October 1969 (FTC *Shinketsushū* 16-46: Yawata Seitestu case). See also S. Imamura, *Dokusen Kinshi Hou* (Anti-Monopoly Law), (Tokyo, 1978) pp 170–173.

There is a simplified procedure for a merger of companies, whose total assets are less than five billion yen. In such mergers, the Fair Trade Commission examines the proposed merger on the basis of the application submitted by the parties. When the market share of any party to the merger, or the combined market share of the parties either (1) reaches or exceeds 25%, (2) is the largest and exceeds 15%, or (3) is the largest and there is a substantial gap between the share of the second or third largest company, close scrutiny is to be given to the proposed merger. The guidelines set out various factors in detail which should be taken into account in examining the proposed merger.[9]

3. CONTROL OF MONOPOLISTIC SITUATION

A new provision concerning 'monopolistic situation' was introduced by the 1977 amendment. According to this provision, when there is a 'monopolistic situation', the Fair Trade Commission may order the entrepreneur to take certain steps, including the transfer of business, and the restoration of a competitive market in goods or services (Art 8-4). This provision is expected to deal with a situation where one or a small number of entrepreneurs dominate the market in any particular market and inhibit free competition.

A situation is regarded as monopolistic, if (1) the market share of one company exceeds 50% or the total share of two companies reaches or exceeds 75%, (2) entry into the market is extremely difficult, (3) there has been a considerable increase in prices, or a decrease in prices has been limited for a certain period and the entrepreneur has either made considerable profits exceeding the norm set by administrative ordinances or has incurred extremely high sales or administration costs (Art 2, s 7).

The Commission is empowered to order the partial transfer of business operations, or assets, the sale of shares, a change in the business methods, and the liberalization of the distribution system. The Fair Trade Commission is required to notify the Minister in charge, if it intends to take such measures. The Minister may present his views to the Fair Trade Commission (Art 45-2). In order to initiate formal proceedings in such cases, a public inquiry must be held. A decision of the Commission shall be reached only with the consent of the chairman and not less than three councillors (Art 55, s 3). The Commission is not allowed to take such an action when (1) the action reduces the scope of a business beyond an appropriate size, (2) it undermines the financial position of the entrepreneur, (3) it makes it difficult to maintain competitiveness in the international market, (4) other measures to restore competition have been taken (Art 8-4, s 1).

It is fairly unlikely that measures to remedy a monopolistic situation will be actually applied, especially the order to transfer part of the operations of a business.[10] The provision is expected to function as a deterrent, especially in relation to a concerted increase in prices led by a dominant entrepreneur. Its actual implementation is considered to be a last resort.

---

[9] Nakagawa, supra, pp 79–83.
[10] Matsushita, supra, pp 95–96.

II. Prohibition of unreasonable restraints on trade

Unreasonable restraints on trade in the sense used by the Anti-Monopoly Law primarily refers to cartels. The Law defines undue restraint on trade as a concerted action of entrepreneurs in mutually limiting or terminating competition in a particular field of trade, which results in substantial restraints on competition, against the public interest (Art 2, s 6). It takes various forms such as the fixing, increasing or maintaining of prices, limiting production outputs, the use of technology, controlling products, facilities, customers, or suppliers. Such undue restraints are prohibited by the Law (Art 3).

One case involved nine companies which supplied coal for brewing. Three sales companies agreed to raise their retail prices. These companies' share of the market virtually reached 100% of the domestic market of this type of coal. The Fair Trade Commission found this agreement to be a substantial restriction on competition for the sale of such coal and ordered its revocation.[11]

Mutual restraint does not have to be legally binding. Even a gentlemen's agreement will suffice in certain cases. There is some debate as to whether the parties should be competitive entrepreneurs, or could they be entrepreneurs without competitive relations. In this regard, whether the Law prohibits 'vertical' agreements as well as 'horizontal' agreements became an issue when newspaper companies and newsagents made a tacit agreement regarding the territory of each agent. The Appellate Court ruled that restraint in the sense of Art 2, s 6 should be mutual, not unilateral, and its content should be the same for all parties. Thus, the court rejected the application of the Anti-Monopoly Law to an agreement of mutual restraint between newspaper companies and newsagents.[12]

It is understood that the agreement does not have to be explicit. In practice, it is often difficult to prove the existence of a mutual agreement among entrepreneurs. It is not sufficient to prove that there was apparently a coincidence of action; a certain correspondence of will is required.[13] There was a case where members of a plywood manufacturers association were invited for tenders by a government agency. The representatives of the companies discussed the bidding price in advance, and the bids coincided. The Fair Trade Commission ruled that the coincidence of the bidding price was not sufficient to prove concerted action, but in this particular case, it acknowledged the existence of such an action, since each company had predicted actions of the other companies and acted with an intention to match their actions.

In a similar case, oil companies made bids for a government purchase. The companies held several meetings of representatives, and 'had a chat' concerning the bidding price. As a result, the prices quoted by the companies showed uniformity. The Fair Trade Commission found this to be a mutual agreement in restraint of trade, and the appellate court upheld this decision.[14]

[11] Recommendatory Decision of the Fair Trade Commission, 28 July 1982.
[12] Judgment of the Tokyo Appellate Court, 9 March 1953 (*Kousai Minshū* 6-9-435: Asahi Shinbun case).
[13] Decision of the Fair Trade Commission, 30 August 1949 (FTC *Shinketsushū* 1-62: Yuasa Mokuzai Kougyou case).
[14] Judgment of the Tokyo Appellate Court, 9 November 1956 (*Gyousaireishū* 7-11-2849: Nihon Sekiyu case).

Some academics assert that if there is a concerted action, and if such action is inconceivable without prearrangement, the existence of such an action itself serves as proof of mutual agreement. However, such a view remains in the minority.[15]

Another problem is related to the widely-utilized instrument of administrative guidance. If a cartel has been formed in response to administrative agency's guidance, does this legitimize the cartel which restrains trade? The Fair Trade Commission has long held the view that the fact that the entrepreneurs followed administrative guidance does not in itself make an illegal cartel legal.[16] This problem was at issue in the celebrated *oil cartel* cases.

In one case, oil companies, which formed the Association of Oil Companies, had been mutually restricting the refinement of crude oil. The ministry which was responsible for formulating and implementing policies concerning the supply of oil products is the Ministry of International Trade and Industry. Control was to be effected by restrictions on the output of oil products. The Ministry implemented its policy of restricting the output by administrative guidance through the existing cartel. The Association of Oil Companies decided the total amount of crude oil to be refined and made corresponding allocations to member companies. The Fair Trade Commission found this cartel to be illegal, and prosecuted the company directors.

The Appellate Court ruled that this restriction on production was against the Anti-Monopoly Law, but acquitted the defendants on the ground that they had not realized that the act was illegal. The court, however, referred obiter dicta to the relationship between administrative guidance and the cartel, and suggested that if the restraints on production had been consequent on the instructions of the Ministry, such action can be justified and should not be regarded as illegal. It also accepted the possibility that actions will be justified, if committed in consequence of the guidance of the Ministry or on its approval.[17]

Another oil price cartel was examined in a case considered before the Supreme Court. The Ministry of International Trade and Industry had set the maximum price for oil products by way of administrative guidance. Oil companies intended to exercise influence over the price and decided to notify the Ministry of the desirable maximum price. In addition, they mutually agreed that once the maximum price was set, they should raise the price to the maximum. The Fair Trade Commission prosecuted directors of the companies for operating an illegal cartel.

The Supreme Court denied that this cartel was based on administrative guidance, and found it to be against the Law. The court stated in obiter dicta that administrative guidance which does not have an explicit legal basis, can be justified, if it is made in a reasonable and socially acceptable way and does not contradict the fundamental purpose of the Anti-Monopoly Law. If it was formed as a consequence of administrative guidance,[18] a cartel on prices which seemingly contravenes Anti-Monopoly Law should not be considered illegal.

---

[15] Matsushita, supra, pp 110–116.
[16] Interpretations on the Relations between the Anti-Monopoly Law and Administrative Guidances, Fair Trade Commission, 16 March 1981. Nakagawa, supra, pp 171–173.
[17] Judgment of the Tokyo Appellate Court, 26 September 1980 (*Kousai Keishū* 33-5-511: the case of Idemitsu Kousan and others).
[18] Judgment of the Supreme Court, 24 February 1984 (*Hanrei Jihou* 1108-3: the Oil Cartel case).

Academic opinion varies on this issue. The majority finds such cartels illegal, even though they were formed as a consequence of administrative guidance. After all, administrative guidance is an act of an administrative agency which does not have the power to give an authoritative interpretation of the Law. If such cartels were to be legitimized only because they had been based upon administrative guidance, it means that administrative agencies are free to create exceptions to the Anti-Monopoly Law.

On the other hand, some lawyers support the position of the Supreme Court. One leading specialist in this field is of the opinion that while the existence of administrative guidance does not in itself justify a cartel, there are cases where restraints on competition by such a cartel do not contradict the ultimate goal of the Anti-Monopoly Law. Such a cartel is not against the public interest as provided by Art 2, s 6, and thus is not illegal. The existence and content of administrative guidance is to be taken into account when judging whether the cartel is against the public interest or not.[19]

The Law also regulates the activities of trade associations—although these do not necessarily fall within the definition of cartels. Trade associations are prohibited from (1) substantially limiting competition in a specific area of trade, (2) entering into international agreements or contracts which are against Art 6, (3) limiting the present or future number of entrepreneurs in a particular field of business, (4) unreasonably restricting the functions or activities of member entrepreneurs, (5) forcing entrepreneurs to employ unfair trade practice (Art 8, s 1). Whether or not the association is a juridical person does not matter.

When a manufacturers' co-operative for school uniforms decided to raise its prices by 20% it notified its members and as a result, the price for most uniforms went up. The Fair Trade Commission found this to be against this provision.[20] In another case, a grocers' co-operative made it a rule that members should not sell goods to retail traders who were not members; it instructed its members who violated this rule to cease such activity. The Fair Trade Commission ordered the co-operative to repeal the rule.[21]

Controlling a concerted increase of prices by major companies is not easy, since it is difficult to prove the existence of an agreement. The Fair Trade Commission had planned to introduce a requirement to disclose production costs when raising prices. This proposal met objections from the companies, and instead, the amendment of 1977 introduced the compulsory reporting of simultaneous price increase in goods or services by those entrepreneurs who have a large share in a particular market. If more than two entrepreneurs, including the one with the largest share in the market, increase prices by the same or similar amount within three months, the Fair Trade Commission may ask these entrepreneurs to file a report explaining the reasons for such price increases (Art 18-2, s 1).[22]

Another novelty concerning the prohibition of cartels is the system of

---

[19] M. Matsushita, supra, pp 122–124.
[20] Recommendatory Decision of the Fair Trade Commission, 29 June 1973 (FTC *Shinketsushū* 20-41: Hifuku Kumiai case).
[21] Recommendatory Decision of the Fair Trade Commission, 13 January 1966 (FTC *Shinketsushū* 13-99: Okazaki Seikashou Kyoudoukumiai case).
[22] Imamura, supra, pp 357–366.

surcharge, which was introduced in the same year. When an entrepreneur exercises unreasonable restraint on trade in relation to the prices, the Fair Trade Commission may impose surcharges (Art 7-2).

III.   Unfair trade practices

The Anti-Monopoly Law prohibits unfair trade practices (Art 19, Art 2, s 9). Unfair trade practices comprise the following acts which are likely to obstruct fair competition and are so designated by the Fair Trade Commission: (1) unjust discrimination against other entrepreneurs, (2) dealing at an unjust price, (3) unjustly soliciting or forcing a competitor's customers to deal with oneself, (4) dealing with another party on terms which unjustly restrict that party's business operations, (5) abusing one's bargaining power in dealings with others, (6) an entrepreneur unjustly obstructing deals between his competitor or a competitor of a company, in which he is a shareholder or a director on one hand, and the competitor's customer on the other hand. Furthermore, the Law prohibits entrepreneurs from unjustly requesting or forcing shareholders or directors to act against the interests of the company, when the competitor is a company (Art 2, s 9). In addition, Art 6, s 1 prohibits entrepreneurs from concluding an international contract which constitutes unfair trade practice.

Unfair trade practices are designated by the Fair Trade Commission in its notices.[23] Thus, the Fair Trade Commission exercises quasi-legislative power in this respect. There are general designations which apply to all industries, and special designations which apply to a specific business. The Notice of 18 June 1982 lists 16 general unfair trade practices.

The prohibition on unfair trade practice is intended to prevent the emergence of private monopolies by regulating acts which may lead to such monopolies. This covers not only unfair methods of competition, but also deceptive practices. It should be added that these provisions concerning unfair trade practices are closely related to consumer-protection legislation. In this regard, the Law against Unjust Premium Advertisement, and Labelling, the Law against Unjust Competition and some other laws also play a significant role. Furthermore, the restriction on unfair trade practice contributes to the protection of entrepreneurs in economically weak positions. This especially applies to the prohibition of abuse of a dominant bargaining position.

The constitutionality of the delegation of legislative power to the Fair Trade Commission was once challenged in the Commission's proceedings. It was argued that such a blanket delegation of legislative power undermined the supremacy of the Diet. The Commission rejected this argument by pointing out that the Law sufficiently specifies the scope of delegation, and besides, restriction of unfair trade practice has to be flexible enough so as to cope with

[23] For example, Fair Trade Commission Notice No 15, 1982. An English version can be found in Nakagawa, supra, pp 63–65.

complicated and changing economic phenomena which were therefore impossible to regulate by means of primary legislation only.[24]

The first category of acts which constitute unfair trade practices covers, among others, (1) the joint refusal of companies to deal with a third company, (2) discriminatory pricing, (3) discrimination in terms of trade. The commonest example of a joint refusal is a boycott. In one case, a refusal by wholesale traders which caused difficulties to a retail trader in finding alternative supplies was ruled to be an unjust refusal, which was likely to inhibit fair competition.[25]

Discriminatory pricing means unjustly supplying or purchasing commodities or services at prices that discriminate between regions or parties. In one case, a manufacturer of floorboards encouraged some builders to join a co-operative in order to maintain the retail price of floorboards. The builders who did not join the co-operative were forced to buy the boards at a higher price. This was found to be discriminatory by the Fair Trade Commission.[26]

The second category of unfair trade practices is unjust pricing. Naturally, selling at a reduced price does not in itself constitute a barrier to fair competition, but if the price is unreasonably reduced in order to eliminate competitors, it is against the Law. In practice, however, it is often difficult to demarcate the boundary between unreasonable and reasonable reductions in prices. The Fair Trade Commission's Notice defines unreasonably low retail prices as involving a continuous supply of goods or services at a price which is excessively below the cost incurred in the said supply, or other kinds of supply at a low price, which are likely to cause difficulties to a competitor's business (s 6).

There was a case where a newspaper company sold papers at 500 yen (approx 4 dollars) for a month's subscription in certain areas in order to attract new readers. Although the price was nominally the same as the cost-price, the Fair Trade Commission ruled that this cost was inconceivable without a subsidy from the parent company. The Tokyo Appellate Court ruled that the price should not only be below market price, but should also be lower than the cost-price, if it is to be considered an unreasonably low price. The court acknowledged that 500 yen was unfair, and ordered the newspaper company not to sell the paper at a price lower than 812 yen.[27]

The third category of unfair trade practice is deceptive soliciting and soliciting by unreasonable benefits. In one case, a company which offered a colour television set to those who had purchased air conditioners from a certain retailer was recommended by the Fair Trade Commission to retract such an offer.[28] The Law prohibits sales by deceptive advertisement or labelling, as well as sales by excessive benefits. As for the latter, in 1962, the Law against Unjust Premiums, Advertisement, and Representation was enacted.[29] The Fair Trade

---

[24] Decision of the Fair Trade Commission, 11 October 1968 (FTC *Shinketsushū* 15-84: Morinaga Shouji case).

[25] Supra, note 21.

[26] Recommendatory Decision of the Fair Trade Commission, February 1980 (FTC *Shinketsushū* 26-85: Touyou Linoleum case).

[27] Decision of the Tokyo Appellate Court, 30 April 1975 (*Kousai Minshū* 28-2-174: Chūbu Yomiuri case); Consentient Decision of the Fair Trade Commission, 24 November 1977 (FTC *Shinketsushū* 24-50).

[28] Recommendatory Decision of the Fair Trade Commission, 6 February 1968 (FTC *Shinketsushū* 14-99: Tsunashima Shouten case).

[29] Law No 134, 1962.

Commission is empowered by this Law to set the maximum of benefits which can be offerred, and also to designate an acceptable form of advertising (Art 2).

In addition to the above-mentioned unfair trade practices, the Anti-Monopoly Law and the notices prohibits 'tie in' sales, dealing on exclusive terms, and the imposition of conditions regarding the retail price. In 'tie in' sales, the seller makes it a condition of sale that the buyer purchase other goods sold by the seller. Dealing on exclusive terms means making it a condition not to deal with competitors. Thus, acts of imposing conditions on deals with others which unjustly limit any of their transactions with a third party are regarded as unfair trade practices (Notice, s 13).

Suppliers of goods often make it a condition of sale that the buyer—mainly retail traders—observe the sales price when reselling the goods. In principle, prices should be determined by the market, and such control of resale prices is considered to be unfair trade practice. The Law provides for some exceptions, but they do not apply when such control of retail prices results in unjust infringement of the interests of consumers (Art 24-2).

Furthermore, impediment of a competitor's business and interference with the internal affairs of a competing company is considered to be an unfair trade practice (Notice, ss 15 & 16).

One of the unique features of Japanese Anti-Monopoly Law lies in the restrictions placed on the abuse of a dominant bargaining position (Art 2, s 9 item 5). It is unlawful, *inter alia*, to force the other party who is in a continuous trade relationship, to purchase related goods or services, to force the other party to offer money, services, or other economic benefits, to impose disadvantageous terms of trade or to change those terms to the disadvantage of the other party. These acts have to be unjust in the light of the normal trade practice and have to be committed by abusing a dominant bargaining power to constitute unfair trade practices. There was a case where a major department store was found to have abused its dominant bargaining position vis-à-vis its suppliers. The department store virtually forced the suppliers to purchase goods and services from the department store and made them pay the cost of refurbishment.[30]

Since the banks tend to hold a superior position vis-à-vis other companies, there were some cases involving banks. In one case, a bank made it a condition of a loan that the managing director and executive directors were to be selected on its instruction. This was acknowledged by the Fair Trade Commission to be an abuse of its dominant bargaining position.[31] In another case, a bank asked a company, which sought a loan, to borrow more money than it needed. The excess amount was to be deposited at the bank. This would enable the bank to gain an unfair interest on the loan. This was also found to be an unfair trade practice.[32]

[30] Consent Decision of the Fair Trade Commission, 17 June 1982 (FTC *Shinketsushū* Mitsukoshi case).

[31] Recommendatory Decision of the Fair Trade Commission, 6 November 1953 (FTC *Shinketsushū* 5-61: Nihon Kougyou Ginkou case).

[32] The Judgment of the Supreme Court, 20 June 1977 (*Minshū* 31-4-449: Gifu Shinyoukumiai case). See also K. Sanekata, 'Banking Transactions and the Anti-Monopoly Law (in Japanese)', in I. Kato et al, eds, *Kinyuu-Torihiki Hou Taikei* (The System of Financial Law), vol 1 (Tokyo, 1983) pp 311–320.

IV. Regulations on international agreement

The Law prohibits entrepreneurs from entering into an international agreement or contract which constitutes an unreasonable restraint on trade or unfair trade practice (Art 6, s 1). The Fair Trade Commission is empowered to order entrepreneurs to rescind such agreements or contracts. Entrepreneurs who have entered into an international agreement or contract are required to file a report with the Fair Trade Commission and submit a copy of such an agreement or contract within 30 days of its conclusion (Art 6, s 2).

In 1972, an international agreement between Japanese and German companies producing rayon was found to be against the Law. In this case, three major Japanese producers of rayon (who controlled the majority share of the domestic market) reached agreement with West German companies. They agreed not to export goods to the others' 'national markets', and mutually limited the amount of exports to their 'common markets' such as the United States. They also agreed to set the minimum sales prices for each country within their 'common market'. The Fair Trade Commission found that this agreement substantially restricted competition in export of rayon. However, it refrained from deciding upon the legality of this international cartel itself and found that three Japanese companies mutually restricted competition in a substantial way and ordered rescission of the agreement.[33] Incidentally, in this case, the Japanese Fair Trade Commission acted in co-ordination with the German Federal Cartel Office. West German companies involved in this agreement were fined by the Cartel Office.

This provision of the Anti-Monopoly Law does not in itself mean that the law can be applied in an extra-territorial way. Japanese law acknowledges extra-territorial application only when there is an explicit provision. However, if an international agreement or contract involving unreasonable restraint on trade or unfair trade practices which was concluded abroad has an effect in Japan, the Japanese Anti-Monopoly Law can be applied to such acts.[34]

The number of formal decisions taken by the Fair Trade Commission concerning international agreements and contracts is small. However, the Commission is said to be relying on administrative guidance without resorting to formal procedures. In this way, the Commission is fairly active in controlling international agreements and contracts.[35]

V. Exemptions

There are exceptions to the provisions of the Anti-Monopoly Law. The Law itself provides for some categories of cases where the provisions of the Law do not apply. In addition, other laws provide for exemptions for various reasons.

[33] Recommendatory Decision of the Fair Trade Commission, 27 December 1972 (FTC *Shinketsushū* 19-124: the case of Asahi Kasei Kougyou and others).
[34] Matsushita, supra, pp 179–180.
[35] Matsushita, supra, p 188.

The Anti-Monopoly Law provides for seven categories of exemptions: (1) railway companies, electricity and gas companies and other companies, which, by virtue of the nature of their business, constitute monopolies, (2) legitimate acts based on specific laws and orders, such as the Law on Local Railways and the Law on Hygiene of Foods, (3) exercise of rights as provided by laws concerning intellectual property, (4) acts of certain kinds of co-operatives, such as consumers' co-operatives, (5) maintenance of resale prices for certain categories of goods, (6) depression cartels, (7) rationalization cartels (Arts 21, 22, 23, 24, 24-2, 24-3, 24-4).

A depression cartel is formed with the authorization of the Fair Trade Commission, when the prices of goods fall below the average costs of production and a majority of producers are likely to discontinue business. This kind of cartel may be formed in order to limit production output, the volume of sales, and production facilities. A rationalization cartel is designed to enhance rationalization of enterprises by taking concerted action, for example, to reduce costs and increase efficiency. Some of these exemptions do not contradict the fundamental aims of the Anti-Monopoly Law, while others are regarded as a 'retreat' from the Anti-Monopoly Law in order to achieve different policy goals.[36]

VI.   Sanctions for violation of the Anti-Monopoly Law

For violations, the Law provides for administrative measures, such as orders to take corrective measures and orders to pay surcharges; civil law measures comprise the payment of compensation; criminal sanctions are also available.

The Fair Trade Commission is empowered to order entrepreneurs to cease violations of the Law, and to take necessary measures to eliminate such violations (Art 7). Such measures range from partial transfers of business operations, transfers of shares, termination of merger plans, deletion of certain clauses from contracts, rescission of agreements and dissolution of cartels. The Commission has to follow a formal quasi-judicial procedure in issuing such orders.

Any person who considers that there has been a violation of the Law is entitled to report the fact to the Fair Trade Commission and request that appropriate action be taken. The Commission is required to conduct an investigation on receipt of such a report. The Commission is also empowered to start investigation *ex officio*. In the course of investigation, the Commission may require (1) witnesses or persons involved to appear for questioning, (2) experts to appear and give evidence, (3) the submission of accounts and other items. The Commission may enter any place of business, or other premises in order to inspect business activities, a company's financial situation and its accounting

---

[36] Imamura, supra, pp 194–209.

records. The Commission may entrust such investigations to its investigators (Art 46, ss 1 & 2).

If, as a result of an investigation, a violation of the Law is found, the Commission either issues a recommendation or initiates formal proceedings. Of the two procedures, the Commission seems to prefer the former. Even when the act in violation of the Law has ceased, the Commission may still recommend that action be taken. In both cases, if the person accepts the recommendation, the Commission may render a recommendatory decision without taking formal proceedings (Art 48).

If there is a violation of the Law and the Commission considers that it is in the public interest to have the case dealt with via formal proceedings, it renders a decision to start formal hearings (Art 49, s 1). Hearings can be conducted either by the Fair Trade Commission or by a Hearings Commissioner (administrative law judge). Most cases are handled by Hearings Commissioners. The hearing is conducted on an adversarial system. An official of the Commission is entrusted with the task of pursuing the charge brought against the respondent. The respondent has the right to be represented by an attorney (Art 52).

The Hearings Commissioner *does not* have the power to render a final decision. When the hearing is completed, he drafts a decision, and sends it to the Commission and the respondent. The respondent may file an objection to the draft. The Commission will take this into consideration and renders a formal decision (Art 54).

If, after the Commission has decided to initiate formal proceedings, the respondent accepts the validity of the facts and the application of law as indicated in this decision, and offers to accept it without a formal hearing, the Commission may render a consent decision. The respondent, in such cases, is required to submit a plan of action which describes the steps he will take in order to remedy the breach of the Law (Art 53-3).

In cases of urgency, where the issuing of such orders could take too long, the Commission may apply to the Tokyo Appellate Court for an injunction (Art 67).

By the 1977 amendment, surcharges were introduced. When an entrepreneur unreasonably restrains trade through the pricing of the goods or services or affects prices by substantially limiting supply of goods or services, or concludes an international agreement or contract to this effect, the Commission is empowered to order the entrepreneur to pay a surcharge. The surcharge is set at one half of the amount obtained by multiplying the amount of sales while the act has been committed by 3% (for manufacturers, 4%, retail traders 2%, wholesale traders, 1%) (Art 7-2). This is designed to deprive the entrepreneur of any excess profit he may have obtained from operating a cartel.

Surcharges were first imposed on concrete companies which had established a joint sales company in a locality and started to supply concrete only to this company. The companies jointly fixed the selling price. The Fair Trade Commission found this to be an unreasonable restraint on trade and ordered the parties involved to pay surcharges.[37]

---

[37] Order to Pay Surcharge of the Fair Trade Commission, 17 August 1978 (FTC *Shinketsushū* 25-51: Asano Concrete case).

Decisions of the Fair Trade Commission can be reviewed by the courts. The Tokyo Appellate Court has an exclusive jurisdiction over such cases. Those who have had their legal interests damaged by a decision have standing to bring the case to court. However, the previous decisions of the Commission and court judgments seem to limit standing. There was a case where a Japanese company concluded an international contract which was against Art 6, s 1 of the Law. The Fair Trade Commission recommended that the company rescind the contract, and the company accepted it. The foreign party to the contract brought the case to court. The Tokyo Appellate Court denied standing to the foreign party, and the Supreme Court upheld this decision. The Supreme Court based its judgment on the ground that the decision of the Commission was not binding on the foreign party, which was a third party to the proceedings, and thus its legal interests had not been damaged.[38]

When the court reviews a decision of the Fair Trade Commission, if it finds that the facts found by the Commission are based on substantial evidence, then it is bound by these facts (Art 80, s 1). The court merely reviews the case on points of law.

The Law also provides that an entrepreneur who has created a private monopoly, unreasonably restrained trade or resorted to unfair trade practices is liable in damages. The entrepreneur cannot be exempted from liability by claiming the absence of intention or negligence (Art 25). For instance, when, as a result of joint refusal to trade by some companies, a company has suffered damage, the latter is entitled to claim compensation from the former. Where consumers have purchased goods or services at a high price maintained by unfair trade practice, the consumers are entitled to claim compensation.[39]

Claims can only be made after a decision has been rendered by the Fair Trade Commission as to the legality of the entrepreneurs' actions has taken effect. The Tokyo Appellate Court has the exclusive jurisdiction over such cases.

The Anti-Monopoly Law also provides for criminal sanctions. A maximum of three years' imprisonment or a fine of five million yen (approximately twenty thousand pounds) can be imposed by the court for various violations of the Law. Only the Fair Trade Commission has the power to initiate the proceedings.

---

[38] Judgment of the Tokyo Appellate Court, 19 May 1951 (*Gyousaireishū* 22-5-761: Amano Seiyaku and Novo Industry case).
[39] Judgment of the Tokyo Appellate Court, 19 September 1977 (*Kousai Minshū* 30-3-247: Matsushita Denki Sangyou case).

Joint ventures with Japanese companies—problems of Anti-Monopoly Law

R Geoffrey Grice

Since Japanese partnership law[1] is relatively undeveloped, it is usual for joint ventures involving Japanese parties to be established as companies rather than as partnerships. If such a joint venture company is to be established in Japan, three principal requirements must be met. These are reports to, and reviews by, the local Legal Affairs Bureau of the Ministry of Justice (commercial recording matters), the Bank of Japan (foreign exchange matters), and the Japanese Fair Trade Commission (anti-trust matters). Apart from certain procedural problems which continue to obfuscate the otherwise routine nature of commercial recording, this paper will concentrate on the latter two requirements.

1. Commercial recording

LEGAL AFFAIRS BUREAU PROCEDURES

If a joint venture is to be established in corporate form then it must be registered as a new company in compliance with Japanese law. Under Art 188 of the Commercial Code (Law No 48 of 1899, as amended), certain details regarding the newly established company must be recorded at the local Legal Affairs Bureau (LAB) of the Ministry of Justice within two weeks after the founding meetings of the company. The principal details to be recorded are as follows: (1) company name, (2) address of its head office, (3) public notification procedures, (4) par value per share, (5) total number of authorized shares, (6) total number of issued shares, (7) amount of capital, (8) reason for and date of recording, (9) business purposes of the company, (10) directors of the company, and other items (eg, that all share transfers are subject to the approval of the board of directors).

BUSINESS PURPOSES CLAUSES

The 'business purposes clause' of a Japanese company's Articles of Incorpora-

---

[1] Arts 667–688, Civil Code.

tion must be drafted in a manner which is acceptable to the officials of the local LAB. They will require a certain level of specificity to comply with the uniform standards of business classification used in Japan. For example, the word 'lease' would be rejected outright, as the LAB always requires 'lease' to be prefaced by words such as 'aircraft', 'motor vehicle' or 'furniture'.

As a company has the authority only to act within the parameters of its Articles of Incorporation[2], the 'business purposes' clause theoretically binds the company as to the extent of its business activities. Companies which have a variety of purposes will rarely state them in detail and if the purposes are stated broadly and abstractly they usually have little restrictive effect. However, since a joint venture company is by its nature established for the purpose of carrying out a certain business, the clause must be drafted to cover precisely the objectives of the joint venture company.

POTENTIAL PROCEDURAL DIFFICULTIES

In addition to the LAB filing, two other procedural steps must be taken. First, before they may be filed with the LAB, the Articles of Incorporation must be notarised by a Japanese notary public, his function being to ensure that the Articles do not violate Japanese law.

Secondly, where it entails an acquisition of shares in a non-listed Japanese company by a 'foreign investor', the establishment of such a joint venture company is classified as a 'direct domestic investment' under the Foreign Exchange and Foreign Trade Control Law (the FEFTCL[3]). Accordingly, the FEFTCL provides that a Notification of Acquisition of Shares must be filed with the Bank of Japan (BOJ). This form includes notification of the wording of the business purposes clause of the proposed company.

Since a 15 day waiting period is imposed on the parties after the Notification is filed with the BOJ, during which time they are unable to proceed with the LAB commercial recording, it is only after BOJ approval is obtained that the LAB recording may be initiated. All too frequently, either the LAB recording is prevented by the notary public refusing to notarise the Articles because the 'business purposes' clause violates the Commercial Code, or the LAB rejects the business purpose clause for not being sufficiently specific. In either case, it is impossible to amend the wording of the submission to the LAB because of the LAB requirement that it be precisely the same as the wording of the BOJ Notification. And since the BOJ Notification may not be amended, the whole procedure must begin again.

Consequently, where such problems are envisaged, or where the degree of specificity required for the 'business purposes' clause is unclear, it is often advisable to ask the LAB to screen the proposed 'business purposes' clause in advance of both the formal commercial recording and the BOJ Notification, to determine whether it will meet with their requirements.

---

[2] Civil Code Art 43 and Commercial Code Art 55.
[3] Law No 226, 1949 as amended.

2. Foreign exchange

THE FOREIGN EXCHANGE AND FOREIGN TRADE CONTROL LAW

In December 1980 substantial amendments were effected to the Foreign Exchange and Foreign Trade Control Law, the law which provides for foreign investment and exchange control in Japan. Prior to these amendments the law had imposed a general prohibition on external transactions with a system of exemptions, notifications, licenses and permits being issued on a case-by-case basis. The 1980 amendments reversed the presumption, and the law now provides for controls only as an exception to the general principle of 'freedom of foreign exchange, foreign trade and other external transactions.' Thus, notification, examination and license requirements are now imposed only if the transaction concerned falls under certain defined exceptions to the general principle of freedom.

Regulation under the FEFTCL varies in accordance with the category of the transaction involved. 'Normal current transactions', based on the transfer of tangible goods or services, are left relatively free of detailed regulation or case-by-case approval requirements. Article 16 ('payments and receipts of payments') of the FEFTCL provides that, except where emergency regulation is necessary, licenses are not needed by residents or non-residents for (i) ordinary service transactions other than those specified in Art 25, which are those that relate to the mining industry or are obstructive of Japan's international treaty commitments, such as the supply of weaponry; (ii) current transactions, such as for travelling overseas or remittances between family members; and (iii) donations, gifts, etc which fall within certain limits. Also expressly excluded are the other categories of transactions defined under the FEFTCL, the most important being 'capital transactions'.

The category 'capital transactions' is defined by Art 20 of the FEFTCL. Essentially, under these transactions only funds change hands. While 'current transactions' entail movements of tangible goods and services, 'capital transactions' do not. As a consequence, 'capital transactions' are perceived as capable of being done 'relatively easily, suddenly, and in large amounts' and for this reason are subject to ad-hoc control under the FEFTCL.

Prior notice is required to be given by residents or non-residents to the Ministry of Finance (MOF) to obtain approval for certain 'capital transactions'. These are specified in Art 23-1 as (i) external monetary loans and guarantees; (ii) direct foreign investments, such as acquisitions of foreign securities or long-term loans to foreign corporations; (iii) issues or offers for subscription of securities in Japan or overseas; and (iv) acquisitions by non-residents of immovable property in Japan. On receipt of such a notice the MOF is empowered to recommend or direct the party to alter the particulars of the transaction or to suspend its execution.

A recommendation will be made where the Ministry views a capital transaction as causing one or more of the adverse consequences specified in Art 23-2 of the FEFTCL. Essentially the criteria employed are of a 'qualitative' nature in that they are not related to the volume or velocity of funds entering or leaving Japan, but are concerned with whether the peculiarity of the transaction may adversely affect the international money market or the smooth performance of the Japanese economy.

For capital transactions other than those specified in Art 23-1, Art 21-1 lists those which are automatically subject to license requirements and Art 21-2 lists those for which the MOF has the discretion to impose license requirements. In contrast with the notice and approval procedures under Art 23-1, these license requirements are to be imposed on a 'blanket' basis rather than in respect of each transaction. For Art 21-2 capital transactions the MOF is empowered to exercise its discretion to prevent the arisal of any of the consequences specified in Art 21-2, consequences which are of a 'quantitative' rather than 'qualitative' nature. Thus, these capital transactions are collectively subject to license requirements where their adverse effect concerns the total volume or velocity of funds crossing the Japanese borders.

The most rigorous control under the FEFTCL is reserved for those transactions which fall within the category of 'direct domestic investments' as defined by Art 26. Although certain transactions may be both 'direct domestic investments' and 'capital transactions', the former are expressly excluded from the definition of 'capital transactions' by Art 20 of the FEFTCL.

For 'direct domestic investments' the Ministry's main objective is the discernment and regulation of the after-effects of the transaction in question. It is directed towards a new category of party, the 'foreign investor', and is aimed to prevent any harmful effects on the relevant area of Japanese industry which might result from the influence that a foreign investor may exert on the Japanese enterprise in which the investment is being made.

'Foreign investor' is broadly defined under the FEFTCL as including non-resident individuals, juridical persons (corporations) established under foreign legislation as well as their branches in Japan, and Japanese juridical persons 'controlled in substance' by foreign individuals or foreign corporations (ie where 50% or more of the stock of such corporations is owned by foreign investors, or where a majority of the directors of such corporations are non-resident natural individuals).

Furthermore, to facilitate effective control, joint jurisdiction is given not just to the MOF and the Ministry of International Trade and Industry (MITI), but also to the other ministries in charge of the industry involved.

'Direct domestic investments' are defined under Art 26-2. Broadly they include (i) acquisitions of shares in any Japanese company which is not a 'listed company'; (ii) acquisitions of shares in any Japanese 'listed company' where such acquisition equals or exceeds 10% of the total issued stock of that company; (iii) establishment by foreign companies of branches in Japan; and (iv) loans to Japanese companies for terms exceeding one year. In addition, Art 29 treats as direct domestic investments and places similar requirements on the conclusion of agreements between residents and non-residents for the importation into Japan of technology. For all such transactions the FEFTCL imposes requirements of notification and approval.

PRIOR NOTIFICATION OF ACQUISITIONS OF SHARES

According to Art 26-3 of the FEFTCL, a foreign investor who intends to acquire shares in a 'non-listed' Japanese company in a 'direct domestic investment' transaction must file a prior notification of such transaction with the MOF and the ministries in charge of the industry involved. This is done by filing a single form with the Bank of Japan (BOJ).

Under Art 26-4, the foreign investor may not carry out the transaction until a specified period of time has passed from the date the notification is filed. Although the statute fixes the waiting period at 30 days, the competent authorities of the BOJ have reduced this period to 15 days.

Upon submission of the notification, the BOJ will take one of three actions. It will either (i) refuse to accept the notification for review, (ii) accept the notification, do nothing, and let the waiting period run, permitting the investment, or (iii) accept the notification, extend the waiting period, and perhaps recommend changes in the investment or, if necessary, order the suspension of the investment. As a practical matter, if the authorities find that the proposed investment is unacceptable for some reason then they will simply refuse to accept it for review. In this way the waiting period never starts to run and they avoid having to take any formal administrative action in connection with the notification.

Review of the notification will be undertaken with regard to the criteria specified in Art 27-1, these being the adverse consequences under which the relevant ministries are empowered to issue a recommendation or directive either to alter the particulars of the transaction or to suspend its execution. These criteria are as follows:

(1) transactions which might pose a threat to national security, disturb the maintenance of public order, or undermine the safety of the general public. This covers those industries exempted from the liberalisation requirements under the OECD's Code of Liberalisation of Capital Movements, such as industries concerned with weaponry, explosives and nuclear power;

(2) transactions which might adversely and materially affect either the activities of Japanese business enterprises engaged in business of a similar nature to that in which the direct domestic investment is to be made, or the efficient performance of the Japanese economy. These industries include the four non-liberalised industries of agriculture and fisheries, mining, oil, and leather and leather product manufacturing;

(3) transactions whose terms are required to be amended or whose execution is delayed because they are made by a foreign investor with whose country Japan has not concluded any treaties or other international agreements providing for reciprocity in the treatment of direct domestic investments; or

(4) transactions whose terms are required to be amended or whose execution is delayed because they constitute, in whole or in part, capital transactions for which a license is required in accordance with the provisions of Art 21-2 of the FEFTCL when viewed in terms of the purpose of the use of funds, etc. This covers attempts to evade emergency restrictions imposed upon capital transactions by use of the guise of direct domestic investments. A good example would be the establishment of a shell company for the speculative purchase of real estate, so that on sale of the land the company may be dissolved with the profits being distributed to the non-resident shareholders.

Once the notification has been filed and the waiting period has run, the foreign or Japanese corporation, as the case may be, will be permitted to acquire the shares of the joint venture company. The foreign or Japanese corporation will thereafter be able to receive dividends, exercise voting rights, and dispose of shares in the company without further intervention by the exchange control authorities.

PRIOR NOTIFICATION OF TECHNICAL ASSISTANCE AGREEMENTS

When a non-resident and a resident intend to conclude or amend an agreement for the transfer of industrial property or other rights concerning technology, for rights to use the same, or for technical assistance, both parties together must file a prior notification of the intended agreement with the BOJ.

The term 'industrial property rights' means patent rights, utility model rights, design rights, and trademark rights which are registered under the applicable laws of Japan (which include the Patent Law, Utility Model Law, Design Law and Trademark Law). The term 'other rights concerning technology' basically means know-how.

According to applicable provisions in the FEFTCL, once the notification has been accepted for consideration by the BOJ, the notifying parties must wait for 30 days before concluding the relevant agreement. For most ordinary types of technology this waiting period has been shortened to one day. Even for specially designated technologies which are deemed to warrant close examination, the waiting period has been shortened to 15 days. These designated technologies include (among others) technologies concerning the manufacture of computers, peripherals for the next generation of computers, lasers and optic fibers, but not telecommunications equipment.

Such notifications are reviewed by the BOJ on behalf of the ministries concerned. If it is considered that any of the adverse consequences specified in Art 30 might result from implementation of the relevant agreement then they are empowered, upon hearing the opinion of the Committee on Foreign Exchange and Other Transactions, to recommend alteration of the particulars of the transaction or the suspension of its execution. The adverse consequences specified in Art 30 are as follows:

(1) transactions which might pose a threat to national security, disturb the maintenance of public order, or undermine the safety of the general public; and

(2) transactions which might adversely and materially affect either the activities of Japanese business enterprises engaged in business of a similar nature to that in which the direct domestic investment is to be made, or the efficient performance of the Japanese economy.

The very broad and vague nature of these standards would appear to allow the Ministry of Finance substantial discretion to interfere with international technology agreements. In fact, however, the BOJ and the competent ministries have rarely raised objections, and these notifications are almost always accepted without amendment.

3. Anti-Monopoly Law

REPORT OF INTERNATIONAL AGREEMENTS TO THE FAIR TRADE COMMISSION

According to the Law on the Prohibition of Private Monopoly and the Maintenance of Fair Trade[4], hereafter the Anti-Monopoly Law, when a Japanese person enters into an international agreement he must file a report of this agreement with the Fair Trade Commission (hereafter FTC) within 30 days of its execution. The concept of an 'international agreement' is not clearly defined in the Law but is interpreted to mean that a 'foreign person' is a party to the agreement. For these purposes, a foreign corporation is considered to be a foreign person, but a Japanese corporation which is wholly-owned by a foreign person is considered to be a domestic person.

In order to be subject to the reporting requirement, the international agreement must be of a duration of one year or greater and must be one of a number of specified categories of agreements. Joint venture agreements are specifically included among the agreements subject to the Anti-Monopoly Law reporting requirements.

The report to be filed must contain detailed information on the parties to the agreement, including a description of their businesses, their capitalisation and their assets. Also, the parties must disclose details of any pre-existing relationships between them, such as equity holdings and personnel connections. In addition, any supplemental agreements between the parties (such as technology transfer agreements and continuous sales agreements) must be disclosed. Information on each party's shareholding in and secondment of personnel to the joint venture must be provided, and the parties must describe any clauses in the joint venture agreement which restrict any business activities of the joint venture, the domestic party or the foreign party.

Upon receiving the report of the joint venture agreement and collateral agreements, the FTC will review the report and the agreements in order to determine if any provisions of these agreements violate the Anti-Monopoly Law. However, it is important to note that this review does not constitute a formal approval process. The FTC may simply review the agreement in a summary fashion and conclude that nothing is violative of the Law. Indeed, the FTC is not required to provide any response at all. Nevertheless, the FTC is not prohibited from raising issues in the future. As a general rule, if the FTC does respond it will do so within about six months of the report being filed.

It is usually recommended that a foreign party insist of the domestic party that the agreements be duly filed and any problems raised by the FTC be resolved as soon as possible in order to avoid any unforeseen difficulties in the

[4] Law No 54, 1947. For and English translation, see M. Nakagawa, *Anti-Monopoly Legislation of Japan* (Tokyo, 1984) pp 3–62.

future. Also, to simplify the processing of the report, it is possible to present the report to the FTC for an informal review prior to actual filing. However, such informal reviews have a tendency to become protracted.

In reviewing the reported agreements, the FTC will consider whether the agreements contain provisions which constitute an 'undue restraint of trade' or an 'unfair business practice', as defined in Art 6(1) of the Anti-Monopoly Law. Certain standards for making these determinations are set forth in a number of FTC memoranda and notices, as follows:

(a) *Unfair Trade Practices Notification* (18 June 1982);

(b) *Unreasonable restraint of trade*: 'Interpretation of Antimonopoly Laws Concerning Export Cartels and International Agreements' (9 August 1972);

(c) *Unfair trade practices*: 'Antimonopoly Law Guidelines for International License Agreements' (24 May 1968); and

(d) *Unfair trade practices*: 'Antimonopoly Law Guidelines for Sole Import Distributorship, Etc, Agreements' (21 November 1972).[5]

Unfortunately, there are no published guidelines concerning joint venture agreements comparable to those concerning international licensing and exclusive distributorship agreements. Of course, if a joint venture agreement were to include such arrangements, then the FTC will review the joint venture agreement under those guidelines.

The FTC will also review a joint venture agreement under Art 3 (monopolization in general) which provides that 'no entrepreneur shall engage in private monopolization ...', which is defined as '... such business activities as are engaged in by any entrepreneur, individually, in combination or conspiracy with other entrepreneurs, or in any other manner, which exclude or control the business activities of other entrepreneurs, thereby causing, contrary to the public interest, a substantial restraint of competition in any particular field of trade.' The two major elements of this prohibition are (a) 'particular field of trade' and (b) 'substantial restraint of competition'. These issues are covered briefly below.

In addition, the FTC will review the shareholding arrangements of the joint venture company in connection with Japanese legal prohibitions of holding companies and restrictions on stock ownership.

If the FTC suspects that any provision in the agreements violate the Anti-Monopoly Law, it will first call the domestic (Japanese) party to explain the reasons for the provision's inclusion, examine the intentions of the parties, and review the background and current status of the matter. It is to be noted that this inquiry might take place immediately after filing or at some future time, pursuant to the FTC's own initiative or following its receipt of a private complaint. Such private complaints are rarely brought by third parties. Usually they are initiated by the Japanese parties to the agreements in the hope that certain terms of those agreements may be avoided.

If the FTC should conclude that one or more of the provisions should be removed from the agreement, then it will make a 'suggestion' in the form of

[5] See Nakagawa, supra, pp 63–65, 124–127.

non-binding 'administrative guidance'[6] (*Gyoshei Shido*) to the domestic party. At this juncture, the suggestion will not be publicly disclosed and has no legal force. In most cases, however, the domestic party will feel compelled to comply.

Should the domestic party refuse to comply, then the FTC may formalise its 'suggestion' by issuing an 'official recommendation' which, if accepted by the domestic party, results in publication of a 'recommendation decision' under Art 48. However, if the domestic party also refuses to accept the 'official recommendation', then the FTC may conduct an official trial of the matter to decide whether to permit the offending provisions or require their removal. The domestic party may appeal against an adverse decision to the Tokyo Appellate Court and from there to the Supreme Court.

As noted above, the party with the obligation to file the report is the domestic party. Foreign parties have no formal standing to appear or appeal during this review process and normally the FTC will not contact the foreign party at the hearing stage. In practice, the FTC may permit the foreign party to appear to express its opinions if it so requests. Consequently, it is always advisable to include in the agreement a provision requiring the Japanese party to allow the foreign party to appear.

In addition, the Japanese courts have held that the FTC action in itself does not affect the validity of the contract or affect the foreign party's rights against the Japanese party for breach of contract. If an action for breach of contract were brought against the Japanese party, then it would be up to the courts to determine whether there had actually been a violation of the AML and, if so, the effect that this would have on the ultimate validity of the contract.

The restricted position of foreign parties with regard to FTC proceedings stems from Novo Industries case[7], which involved an appeal by the foreign party to an international distributorship agreement against an Art 48 'recommendation decision' by the FTC. The recommendatory decision had been issued to the domestic party, Amano Pharmaceutical Co, requiring it to delete a clause which purported to oblige Amano not to manufacture or sell competitive products for three years after the date of termination of the agreement with Novo Industries. Novo's petition to cancel the FTC's 'recommendation decision' was dismissed by the Tokyo Appellate Court without an examination of the merits because Novo could not obtain any legal benefit from the action. It was held that since the FTC 'recommendation decision' was concerned with criminal sanctions under the AML, it had no direct legal effect on the relationship between the two private parties under their contract.

An appeal to the Supreme Court was also dismissed, but on different grounds. That court held that since the 'recommendation decision' was issued without any formal trial procedure it could be enforced by the FTC only through the addressee (the domestic party) voluntarily accepting the 'recommendation decision.' Being based on the will of the addressee to accept it, the 'recommendation decision' could not be regarded as having any binding effect on any third party.[8]

[6] H. Shiono, 'Administrative Guidance' in K. Tsuji, ed, *Public Administration in Japan* (Tokyo, 1984) pp 203–216.

[7] Judgment of the Tokyo Appellate Court, 19 May 1951 (*Gyousaireishū* 22-5-761: Amano Seiyaku and Novo Industry case).

[8] Judgment of the Supreme Court, 28 November 1975 (*Minshū* 29-10-1592: Amano Seiyaku case).

Thus, the effect of this case is to deny any standing for a foreign party to appeal against an accepted recommendatory decision. As a 'Catch 22' it is doubtful whether, in a separate private suit brought in Japan against the Japanese party, the foreign party could obtain either injunctive relief to prevent the former from acting, or damages for acting in breach of the offending provision. Consequently, it is essential to provide in the joint venture agreement a contractual right allowing the foreign party to participate with the Japanese party in negotiations with the FTC.

PROHIBITION OF PRIVATE MONOPOLISATION

As noted above, Art 3 of the Anti-Monopoly Law prohibits private monopolisation and substantial restraints of competition in any particular field of trade.

Article 2(5) of the Law defines the term 'private monopolisation' as the act or acts of 'any entrepreneur, individually, or in combination or conspiracy with other entrepreneurs, or in any other manner, which excludes or controls the business activities of other entrepreneurs, thereby causing, contrary to the public interest, substantial restraint to competition in any particular field of trade.' Thus, the prohibition is aimed not at the 'situation' or private monopolisation, but at the 'conduct' employed towards its achievement. While ordinary business efforts are permitted under Art 3, conduct entailing exclusion or control of other entrepreneurs is absolutely prohibited.

Before analysing the above provisions it should be noted that elsewhere in the Law the FTC is empowered to act against 'monopolistic situations'. Under Art 8-4, an enterprise which has achieved a monopolistic situation in the normal course of business activities and without any aggressive conduct may nonetheless be ordered by the FTC to transfer part of its business to a third party or take other remedial measures. In contrast with Art 3, the prohibition under Art 8-4 is limited to circumstances where (1) the market share of the entrepreneur is over 50% (or 75% for two entrepreneurs); (2) entrance by competitors is considered to be extremely difficult; and (3) the prices of the relevant goods or services have increased remarkably or decreased marginally over a period of time causing the entrepreneur concerned to gain excessive profits or sustain high selling costs. Article 8-4 is further restricted in that the FTC cannot require transfer of part of the enterprise concerned without first consulting with the competent ministries in charge of the relevant industry and then conducting a public hearing on the matter.

The Art 3 prohibition of private monopolistic 'conduct' is subject to no such restrictions. Central to this 'conduct' prohibition is the phrase 'excludes or controls'. This covers situations where the unilateral or combined actions of one or more entrepreneurs imposes restraints on the commercial freedom of other entrepreneurs to such an extent that the latter are prevented from competing, or are able to compete but only on the terms of the former entrepreneurs.

In the Yukijirushi-Nyūgyo Case[9] the FTC decided that a dairy company acting in concert with a financial institution had violated the AML by 'excluding' competitors from collecting fresh milk. On the other hand, in the

[9] Decision of the FTC, 28 July 1954 (*Shinketsushū* 8-12: Yukijirushi Nyūgyou case).

Noda Shouyu Case[10] the FTC decided that a leading soya sauce manufacturer had contravened the AML by 'controlling' the pricing of its competitors through maintaining its resale prices.

Interpretation by the various courts and the FTC of the phrase 'contrary to the public interest' has established that this need not be proved in any particular case since, in principle, any substantial restraint of trade must in itself be contrary to the public interest.

The Tokyo High Court defined the phrase 'substantial restraint of competition' to mean 'bringing about a situation where competition itself declines and a particular entrepreneur or group of entrepreneurs is able to control the market by wilfully and freely manipulating such business conditions as pricing, quality, and volume of supply. The question of what circumstances must exist to demonstrate that market control does exist is a relative problem for which no uniform criteria can be established since it cannot be considered in isolation from the prevailing economic conditions at the time. Market control cannot be determined simply by the volume of supply to the market by the entrepreneur in question.'[11]

Similarly, the determination of the 'particular field of trade' depends upon an exhaustive analysis of the relevant facts. Relevant facts would include the place or the market area in which the relevant companies engage in business, the type of products or services which the relevant companies provide, the breadth of the market, the types of industries involved, differences between the parties to the transaction and numerous other factors.

Despite these difficulties, the FTC has taken the position that in most cases a company will be considered to have achieved the ability to exert market control when it achieves a market share of 25–30%. However, in direct contrast, the Supreme Court stated in the Touhou-Subaru Case in 1959 that 'decisions should be made on a case-by-case basis taking into specific consideration the line of business in question, market conditions, the state of competition and all other relevant facts and circumstances.'[12] Therefore, any technical violation of the FTC figures should not of itself constitute a violation of the Anti-Monopoly Law. Rather, the FTC's position represents only the level of market share at which the FTC will closely scrutinize the transaction.

RESTRICTION ON STOCKHOLDING BY A COMPANY AND ANNUAL REPORT FILING REQUIREMENTS

Article 10 of the Anti-Monopoly Law prohibits the acquisition or holding of stock of a Japanese company if the effect of such acquisition or holding may be to 'substantially restrain competition' in any particular field of trade. Article 10 also prohibits the acquisition or holding of stock which is effected by means of an unfair trade practice.

Parenthetically, it should be noted that Art 9(1) of the Law prohibits the establishment of a holding company in Japan. Also, Art 9(2) prohibits foreign

---

[10] Decision of the FTC, 27 December 1955 (*Shinketsushū* 7–108: Noda Shouyu case).
[11] Judgment of the Tokyo Appellate Court, 7 December 1953 (*Gyoushū* 4-12-3215: Touhou-Shintouhou case).
[12] Decision of the Supreme Court, 25 May 1959 (*Minshū* 8-5-950: Touhou-Subaru case).

companies from operating as holding companies in Japan. The latter would include foreign companies established solely to act as parent companies of joint venture companies in Japan.

In order to monitor such shareholdings, the FTC requires (i) every non-financial domestic corporation whose total assets exceed two billion yen and (ii) every non-financial foreign corporation to file an annual report of such shareholding with the FTC within three months after the end of each business year.

The standards used by the FTC to determine whether the acquisition or holding of shares may 'substantially restrain competition' are similar to those described above. In 1981 the FTC published a detailed set of criteria under which it will make such a determination.[13]

Based upon the authority of the Shirokiya Case[14] decided in 1953, the FTC will order that the party violating Art 10 be prohibited from exercising any voting rights in the shares until the violation has been cured. According to Japanese case law, the underlying acquisition of shares leading to the violation will, however, be held to constitute a valid transaction and the owner will be regarded as the lawful owner of the shares with the right to enjoy the benefits of the shares, subject to the order by the FTC to divest the shares and refrain from exercising voting rights.

RESTRICTIONS ON MERGERS, CONSOLIDATIONS, AND ACQUISITIONS OF BUSINESSES

A merger, consolidation or other similar act is prohibited by the Anti-Monopoly Law Art 15 if its effect may be substantially to restrain competition in any particular field of trade, or if unfair business practices have been employed in the course of the merger, consolidation, or other similar act. The phrase 'other similar acts' includes the acts of acquiring, assuming the lease of, or undertaking the management of, the whole or a substantial part of the business in Japan of another company, or entering into a contract with another company which provides for a joint profit and loss account for business in Japan. It is conceivable that a joint venture (depending upon the facts) could fall within one of these categories.

At least 30 days prior to the date of a transaction described above, a notification of the transaction must be filed with the FTC. The FTC will review the proposed transaction to ensure it does not violate the Anti-Monopoly Law. A set of standards applicable to such a review were published by the FTC in 1980. If necessary, the 30 day waiting period may be extended by the FTC, which will delay the date of the transaction, but any action by the FTC must be taken within such period unless a false or misleading statement has been made in the parties' notification.

---

[13] Nakagawa, supra, pp 89–94.
[14] Judgment of the Tokyo Appellate Court, 1 December 1953 (*Kakyū Minshū* 4-12-1791: Shirokiya case).

4. Problems under the Anti-Monopoly Law

EXCLUSIVE DISTRIBUTION AND THE ANTI-MONOPOLY LAW

Very often one of the main incentives for establishing a joint venture in Japan is to enable, in return for providing advanced technology, the foreign parent company to retain exclusive distribution rights for sales outside Japan of the products manufactured by the joint venture company. For such rights to be effective it is necessary that they do not violate the Anti-Monopoly Law. Here the key consideration is whether it would be illegal to include an exclusive distribution provision in the joint venture agreement or in a technology license contract concluded between the joint venture company and the foreign parent company. If this were to cause the foreign parent company to be the exclusive distributor for the joint venture company's products outside Japan then such exclusivity would entail a restriction on the areas and the persons to whom the joint venture company could export. Consequently, on the filing of these contracts the FTC will scrutinize the legality of these restrictions under the Anti-Monopoly Law.

Both of these points are treated in the FTC's 1968 Antimonopoly Law Guidelines for International Licensing Agreements, the pertinent guidelines being as follows:

> In international licensing agreements or contracts which involve the licensing of patent rights or utility model rights (hereinafter 'patent rights'), the following restrictions are particularly likely to constitute an unfair trade practice:
>
> (1) Restricting the territory to which the licensee may export products covered by the patent or utility model rights (hereinafter referred to as 'patented products'), with the exception of the following instances:
>
> (a) Where the licensor has registered patent rights in the territory to which export by the licensee is restricted (hereinafter referred to as the 'restricted territory');
> (b) Where the licensor sells the patented products on an ongoing basis in the restricted territory; and
> (c) Where the licensor has granted an exclusive sales license to a third party in the restricted territory.
> (5) Making it obligatory for the licensee to sell the patented products through the licensor or a person designated by the licensor.[15]

Item (5) specifically applies to restrictions against the persons to whom the licensee may sell within Japan. It does not apply to restrictions on the licensee's sales to persons outside Japan. The FTC also takes the position, however, that the type of restriction contemplated in this case may fall under item (1), the prohibition on export restrictions. Even though the proposed prohibition does not prevent the joint venture company from exporting its products, it would

---

[15] Nakagawa, supra, pp 79–83.

prevent the joint venture company from exporting its products 'freely'. In this sense, an appointment of the foreign parent company as the exclusive distributor for the joint venture company outside Japan may be viewed in substance as a type of export limitation.

However, even if the proposed exclusive distribution provision were viewed by the FTC as an export restriction, item (1) allows three circumstances in which such restrictions are expressly permitted. These three cases are where either the licensor has patent rights in the restricted area; the licensor already sells the licensed products in the restricted area; or the licensor already has an exclusive licensee or distributor in the restricted area. Even a complete restriction on exports from Japan is permitted in these three cases. This guideline prohibition and its exceptions also apply in cases of know-how and trademark licenses. Therefore, if the foreign parent company as licensor were able to prove that one or more of these three cases existed prior to the conclusion of the exclusive distribution contract, then the legality of such provisions could not be challenged by the FTC.

This result obtains regardless of whether the relevant restriction is contained in the joint venture agreement directly or in a license agreement between the foreign parent company and the joint venture company concluded pursuant to the joint venture agreement. Since this restriction would be fully legal at that time, it would of course also be legal if mentioned in the preamble of subsequent sales agreements.

If exclusive distribution provisions are contained in the joint venture agreement then filing of the agreement with the FTC must be completed by the prospective Japanese parent corporation. If contained in a licensing agreement then the filing must be completed by the joint venture company. In either case, the normal approach is for the parties to agree that if the FTC rejects the foreign parent company's claim of exemption, either in whole or in part, then at that time either the foreign parent company will agree to a final compromise negotiated with the FTC, or the agreement will be terminated. It should also be noted that until the FTC formally questions the exclusive distribution provision it is not necessary for the foreign parent company to provide proof of its claim to qualification under the applicable exemptions.

However, where the filing is of the joint venture agreement and hence is being undertaken by the prospective Japanese parent corporation, it is sometimes the case that prior to filing the prospective Japanese parent corporation will request the foreign parent company to provide proof of qualification under all three cases of exemption, and sometimes even with regard to each country outside Japan. If such a request is received then it should be considered with caution, for it may be interpreted as resistance to the joint venture itself.

ENFORCEABILITY OF NON-COMPETITION PROVISIONS

Contained in the 'International Contract' notification form that is filed with the FTC are questions asking whether in the joint venture (international) agreement there are clauses which restrict the operation of business in competition with parties to the joint venture, including the joint venture company. The notification form requires the applicants to specify any provision in the agreement which purports to restrict competition with the joint venture company or with either parent company (or their subsidiaries and affiliated companies), and it further requires that the party which imposed these restrictions be identified.

These matters concern the non-competition provisions of the Anti-Monopoly Law. In the absence of FTC guidelines dealing specifically with international (joint venture) contracts, the position of the FTC can be seen from its guidelines on non-competition provisions contained in licensing agreements. However, this position has been changing recently towards a more restrictive implementation of the Anti-Monopoly Law.

The position held by the FTC in the past was as follows. In the event that an agreement is terminated due to a breach by a licensee, then the licensor may forbid the licensee to handle any competitive goods for a period of two years following the termination of the agreement or for the period of time the agreement could have remained in effect if it had not been terminated, whichever is the shorter. Recently, the FTC's position on such non-competition restraints has changed. According to recent practice of the FTC, any non-competition provision which purports to be effective after the termination of an agreement violates the Anti-Monopoly Law.

In view of the fact that the FTC's position, both past and present, is one of administrative guidance, and that this guidance has not been the subject of any judicial decision, the legal basis of the FTC's interpretation of the Anti-Monopoly Law is not certain. Furthermore, the uncertainties are compounded by the necessity of reading the international contract provisions in the light of the FTC's position on licensing agreements.

The resulting situation is not satisfactory. If the joint venture agreement contains no non-competition provision whatsoever then no problems should be encountered in this respect on filing with the FTC. However, if the joint venture agreement provides that the Japanese parent corporation shall be subject to two year's non-competition if it should cause the agreement to be terminated by its acting in breach of its terms, then the FTC may apply its present interpretation of the Anti-Monopoly Law and require deletion of the offending provision. Until the FTC's interpretation is challenged on the judicial level this area will remain the subject of considerable uncertainty. No such challenge is expected to occur in the near future.

For the prospective foreign parent company the FTC's restrictive interpretation of the Anti-Monopoly Law poses a distinct threat to the commercial viability of certain types of joint venture in Japan. In effect, it is inviting Japanese corporations to import foreign technology through the medium of joint ventures and then intentionally to breach those joint venture agreements with impunity, so that on termination of the agreements the Japanese corporations can themselves utilize that technology.

Trade friction and the anti-monopoly legislation of Japan—activities of the Fair Trade Commission

M Nakagawa
Administrative Law Judge
Fair Trade Commission of Japan

As early as May 1982, in order to cope with the trade friction problems, the Japanese government decided on a second trade package, a comprehensive set of measures for further opening up Japanese markets.[1] The package included measures to keep a close watch over the distribution channels for imported goods and to apply strictly and properly the Anti-Monopoly Law to any anti-competitive conduct. In line with these measures, the Fair Trade Commission of Japan carried out: (1) close investigation of import related cases, (2) surveys of distribution channels, and (3) surveys of business groups, etc.

In July 1985, the Japanese government produced an action-programme for improved market access, which was designed to open up and liberalize Japanese markets further. On 19 November 1985, the Fair Trade Commission released a basic policy statement entitled 'The Trade Friction Problem'. The statement included three particular areas in the commission's activities, these being:

(1) measures to control import-restricting conducts,
(2) strict control of cartels exempted from the Anti-Monopoly Law, and
(3) surveys on distribution within Japan.

In May 1986, based on the results of a series of surveys, the Fair Trade Commission revised its approach and issued a statement entitled 'Competition Policy Measures for Improved Market Access'. In April 1987, the Commission issued a progress report on its activities carried out in line with this approach.

I. The basic framework of the Japanese Anti-Monopoly Law

Japanese Anti-Monopoly legislation consists of an Anti-Monopoly Law[2] and

---

[1] Regarding the trade issues between the United States and Japan and the Anti-Monopoly Law, see M. Matsushita, 'A Japanese View of United States Trade Laws', *Northwestern Journal of International Law and Business* (Spring, 1987) pp 43–58.
[2] Law No 54, 1947. An English translation is available in M. Nakagawa, *Anti-Monopoly Legislation of Japan* (Tokyo, 1984) pp 3–62.

two supplementary Laws, ie the Subcontract[3] Law and the Law against Unjust Premiums Advertisement and Representations Law (hereafter Premiums and Representations Law).[4]

The Anti-Monopoly Law is designed to promote free and fair competition, to stimulate the creative initiative of entrepreneurs and thereby to promote the democratic and wholesome development of the national economy as well as to assure the interests of consumers in general (Art 1). Thus, it aims to promote efficient competition, ie competition in terms of lowering the price and heightening quality of goods or services. Putting it another way, it aims to maintain and foster an economic environment where goods or services superior in terms of price and quality can easily penetrate markets and gain a proper share consistent with their competitive merits.

In order to achieve these aims, the Law provides for various preventative and prohibitory measures. They can be categorized in three types: (1) measures against the excessive concentration of economic power, (2) measures for the elimination of substantial restraints of competition, and (3) measures against barriers to fair competition.[5]

As regards the first category, the Law provides for corrective measures against monopolistic situations (Art 8-4), restrictions on total amount of stockholding by a non-financial conglomerates (Art 9-2) and restrictions on stockholding rate by a financial company (Art 11). The Law further prohibits the establishment and operation of holding companies. A holding company denotes a company the principal business of which is to control, through the holding of shares, business activities of other companies established in Japan (Art 9). The Law also prohibits shareholding, mergers, interlocking directorates or acquisition of business by a company where it may substantially restrain competition in any particular field of trade (Arts 10, 15, 13 and 16).

Concerning the measures for the elimination of substantial restraint of competition, the Anti-Monopoly Law prohibits Private monopolization (Art 2, s 5, and Art 3), unreasonable restraint on trade (illegal cartel) (Art 2, s 6 and Art 3), specified acts of a trade association (Art 8, s 1 (1)), and international agreements or contracts containing provisions that constitute an unreasonable restraint of trade (or unfair trade practices) (Art 6). In addition to these measures, a surcharge system levied on profits made by illegal cartels was introduced in 1977 (Arts 7-2 and 8-3).

As regards measures against barriers to fair competition, the Law prohibits unfair trade practices (Art 19). Unfair trade practices means 'any act which tends to inhibit fair competition and which is designated by the Fair Trade Commission as such'. These include:

 (i) Unjustly discriminating against other entrepreneurs
 (ii) Dealing at unjust prices
(iii) Unjustly inducing or coercing customers of a competitor to deal with oneself
(iv) Dealing with another party on such terms as will restrict unjustly the business activities of that party

---

[3] Law No 120, 1956. For an English translation, see Nakagawa, supra, pp 177–186.
[4] Law No 134, 1962. For an English translation, see Nakagawa, supra, pp 187–193.
[5] Nakagawa, supra, pp 301–334.

(v) Dealing with another party by unjust use of one's bargaining position
(vi) Unjustly interfering with a transaction of a competitor of an entrepreneur or of a company of which the entrepreneur is a shareholder or a board member, with other parties; or, where such an entrepreneur is a company, unjustly inducing, instigating, or coercing a stockholder or an officer of such company to act against the interests of such company' (Art 2, s 9).

In addition to the Anti-Monopoly Law, there are two more Laws to be mentioned.

The Subcontract Law aims to control abusive conduct of large companies in the manufacturing or repairing work contracts with sub-contractors, and to make transactions of parent entrepreneurs with sub-contractors fair. By protecting the interests of the sub-contractors, the Law is expected to contribute to the wholesome development of the national economy. The following types of conduct by a parent entrepreneur against his sub-contractors are prohibited by the Subcontract Law: (i) unjust refusal to accept the work done; (ii) unjust delay in payment; (iii) unjust return of work done; (iv) unjust fixing of sub-contract rates at a conspicuously low level; (v) the coerced purchase of designated items, and (vi) unjust retaliation. Thus, the Subcontract Law is targeted against the abuse of a dominant bargaining position generally held by large companies.

The Premiums and Representations Law regulates the main types of deceptive customer-inducement, that is, misleading representations to consumers and customer-inducement by unjust benefits, such as excessive premium offers to retail sellers or consumers. The Law also provides for a 'Fair Competition Code'. The 'Fair Competition Code' is a code which entrepreneurs or a trade association may, upon obtaining authorization from the Fair Trade Commission, establish on premiums or representations, in order to prevent unjust inducements and maintain fair competition. There are now over 130 Fair Competition Codes authorized in industries such as the home electric appliances industry, the automobile industry and the chocolate industry.

II. Trade frictions and activities of the Fair Trade Commission

1. FOREIGN NATIONS' CLAIMS AGAINST BARRIERS OF ACCESS TO JAPANESE MARKETS

It was claimed in a series of discussions on trade issues with foreign nations that some of the Japanese market conditions, trade practices, and government policies have in effect hindered the distribution of imported goods or the sales activities of foreign entrepreneurs in Japan. The opportunity of foreign entrepreneurs to compete freely and fairly was allegedly limited in the Japanese market.

These claims can be summarized in the following way:

(1) The following conduct has resulted in import restriction;
  (i) import restricting cartels among importers, Japanese manufacturers and their trade associations,
  (ii) cartels exempted from Anti-Monopoly Law, and
  (iii) so called 'manufacturer importation', a system whereby a competing Japanese manufacturer becomes the sole import distributor of foreign branded goods, simultaneously preventing parallel importations by sole import distributors.

(2) The following factors in the Japanese distribution system have inhibited foreign sales to Japan and resulted in import restricting effects;
  (i) distribution channelization by powerful Japanese manufacturers,
  (ii) rebates paid by powerful Japanese manufacturers to retailers in order to restrain competing goods,
  (iii) strict legal restrictions on premium offers excessively limiting foreign entrepreneurs' sales activities,
  (iv) regulations on representations concerning the country of origin and comparative advertising which inhibit effective advertising and sale of imported goods.

(3) The following trade practices in the Japanese market place burdens on foreign entrepreneurs which have import-restricting effects;
  (i) a tendency to provide less documentation on the conditions of transactions or contracts than in the United States and Europe, and
  (ii) other practices, such as return of unsold goods by retailers, and secondment of sales personnel to retailers from suppliers.

Thus, other countries criticize Japan because of the impression that Japan allows market conditions and trade practices which inevitably work to the advantage of Japanese entrepreneurs and to the disadvantage of foreign entrepreneurs. These conditions are said to have hindered the access of foreign entrepreneurs to the Japanese market, while Japanese entrepreneurs have expanded their share in foreign markets enjoying free and fair competitive market conditions maintained there by those foreign countries.

However, the real source of trade frictions seems to be Japan's huge trade surplus. One of the solutions is to expand Japan's import of manufactured goods through improved market access and increased domestic demand.

The Fair Trade Commission recognized that the entry of foreign entrepreneurs and the importation of foreign manufactured goods are effective means of stimulating competition in the Japanese market. Removing the factors which hinder the access of goods produced by foreign entrepreneurs to the Japanese market is regarded as an important element of the competition policy. On the other hand, it is considered to be necessary to promote international understanding by clarifying Japanese market conditions and trade practices.

2. THE FAIR TRADE COMMISSION'S APPROACH TO MAY 1986[6]

Since the announcement of its basic policy stance on the trade friction problem

[6] FTC, *Annual Report of Japan on Restricted Business Practices for 1986* (Tokyo, 1987) pp 4–14.

in November 1985 to May 1986, the Commission carried out the following fact-finding surveys of the Japanese market regarding possible market-access barriers:

(i) A Survey on Import-Related Trade Associations.
A survey of 27 import-related trade associations was carried out to ascertain the level of membership of foreign entrepreneurs and the compilation of supply and demand forecasts and other information-gathering activities.

(ii) A Survey on the Distribution of Paper Products.
A survey was conducted on various aspects of the paper industry, including the distribution system, the rigidity of trade relations between paper manufacturers and distributors and their financial relationships.

(iii) A Survey on the Trade Practices in the Department Store and Chain Store Industry Relating to Imported Goods.
A survey of nine major department stores and nine major chain-stores was conducted to assess their handling of imported goods, the clarity of conditions of transactions, the practice of returning unsold goods and the practice of suppliers seconding sales personnel to retailers.

(iv) A Survey on Trade Practices in the Distribution of Toiletries and Cosmetics.
A survey of major manufacturers, wholesalers and retailers was conducted to access various aspects of the industry, including imports distribution systems, conditions of transactions, rebates, the practice of returning unsold goods and the practice of suppliers seconding sales personnel to retailers.

In addition, a report entitled 'An International Comparison of Distribution Structures and Trade Practices and Competition Policies' was presented to the Fair Trade Commission in April 1986 by the International Comparative Study Group on Distribution Structures and Trade Practices, which is a research panel of experts. Taking into account international differences in the field of distribution, the report made a number of policy recommendations to the Commission regarding those aspects of the Japanese market considered problematic in relation to competition policy. These included manufacturer-affiliated distribution channelization, the practice of returning unsold goods, rebates, premium offers, and information networking among other things.

Based on the findings of these surveys and research, as well as claims which had been raised regarding FTC-imposed regulations, the Fair Trade Commission put its action areas for market access improvement into four categories listed below, studied each category, and, in May 1986, issued its updated measures under the heading 'Competition Policy Measures for Improved Markets Access'. These cover:

(i) Import-restricting conduct in violation of the Anti-Monopoly Law,
(ii) Cartels exempted from the Anti-Monopoly Law,
(iii) Activities of import-related trade associations, and
(iv) Activities relating to market entry at the distribution level (manufacturer-affiliated distribution channelization, rebates, the practice of returning

unsold goods, that of seconding sales personnel, etc), regulations under the Premiums and Representations Law and sole-import distributorships.

(i) Measures against import restricting conduct

The Fair Trade Commission has strengthened its machinery for collecting information about barriers for access to the Japanese markets for foreign entrepreneurs and goods. It is expected to proceed with its surveillance of conduct in restraint of import. The Commission places special emphasis on detecting any signs of conduct hindering parallel imports.

When the Commission detects any signs of import-restricting conduct, it carries out any necessary investigations. If violations are found, the Fair Trade Commission will take steps to eliminate them and remedy the situation. These steps will be followed up with stringent surveillance.

In line with this measure the Commission has so far carried out two investigations. One is an investigation on the alleged cartel for restriction on imports of soda ash from the United States. It was found that four major Japanese soda ash manufacturers colluded in determining import volumes, transaction ratios and import channels of soda ash from the United States in violation of Art 3 of the Anti-Monopoly Law. The Fair Trade Commission issued a recommendation for elimination of this conduct and the manufacturers accepted it. A recommendation decision was rendered on 31 March 1983. Since then, the Commission has kept surveillance on soda ash imports.

The other case is investigation of the alleged cartel for restricting Styren Butadien Rubger (a kind of synthetic rubber) imports from Taiwan. It was suspected that domestic synthetic rubber manufacturers were restricting import volumes and import channels of SBR from Taiwan. The evidence was, however, not sufficient to sustain the case. Therefore, in July 1984, the Fair Trade Commission issued a strict warning to the manufacturers involved that they risked contravening Arts 3 and 19 of the Anti-Monopoly Law and that they should take the necessary steps to eliminate this suspicion. Since the warning, the Fair Trade Commission has also kept surveillance on synthetic rubber imports.

(ii) Stricter approach to exempted cartels

The Fair Trade Commission has been closely scrutinizing the operations of exempted cartels and has been dealing stringently with these cartels, which are allowed only under certain limited conditions as exceptions out of specific policy objectives.

As at the end of March 1987, the number of cartels implemented under the provisions of Laws other than the Anti-Monopoly Law stood at 382, covering 98 items (the corresponding figures for the end of April 1986 were 422 and 98; those for the end of October 1985, were 433 and 103). The number of such cases has been declining since fiscal year 1972, when there were a total of 979 cartels covering 285 items.[7]

---

[7] A list of exemptions are provided in Nakagawa, supra, pp 215–218.

Most of these cartels either control domestic services or regulate exports in order to prevent trade problems. Others cope with small and medium-sized enterprises affected by recession. These cartels do not relate to importation except for cartels covering two items established in order to counteract foreign government or private actions intended to unify trading channels for export into Japan.

The Fair Trade Commission intends to continue to adopt a rigorous approach to such exempted cartels to ensure that they are not employed too readily.

Regarding voluntary export restraints, the Fair Trade Commission maintains the following position:

a. Voluntary export restraints and production adjustments through such methods as compiling and publishing supply and demand forecasts constrain free production and export activities of entrepreneurs, and therefore they are basically undesirable. However, there are cases where voluntary export restraints and production adjustments are, depending on the economic and social situations of the importing countries, temporarily inevitable for maintaining the free trade system through regulating excessive exports or avoiding dumping problems.

b. Therefore, the Commission has kept close contacts with the ministries concerned about voluntary export restraints and the proper enforcement of the Export and Import Trading Law and The Export and Import Trading Control Ordinance, which are used to control such restraints. The Commission has paid attention to whether the restraint was actually limited to the necessary minimum and did not distort competition in the domestic markets.

(iii) Surveillance of the activities of import-related trade associations

Trade associations carry out various activities to promote common interests of their members. Such activities include management advice and supply of information to the members. Effective business operation of an entrepreneur may be difficult if he is unable to join a relevant trade association.

The above-mentioned survey on 27 import-related trade associations revealed that none of them discriminated against foreign entrepreneurs regarding the eligibility for membership or admission procedures. The Fair Trade Commission will, however, continue surveillance of import-related trade associations in order to prevent such cases.

In principle, the Fair Trade Commission does not consider the compilation and publication of supply and demand forecasts based on past import and sales statistics, the production of future supplies and demand trends and other indicators to be a problem. The Commission, however, intends to take necessary measures such as requesting correction of such forecasts, which may have an import-restricting effect or raise suspicions that they are compiled with the aim of restricting imports. These include cases:

a. where a trade association compiles supply and demand forecasts of very short range,

b. where a trade association compiles supply and demand forecasts directly using the members' own forecasts, and/or
c. where the membership of the association compiling the forecasts includes domestic manufacturers that produce goods similar to the relevant imports.

The Fair Trade Commission also intends to adopt a strict approach to cases where import-restricting effects may result from the exchange of information on import prices, import volumes or sales channels, the solicitation of reports from the members about planned import volumes and consultation with domestic manufacturers' associations regarding import volumes.

(iv) Maintenance and promotion of the openness of the market for distribution

The Fair Trade Commission has so far endeavoured to maintain competitive conditions conducive to market entry through the elimination of trade practices which inhibit fair and free competition in the field of distribution. The Commission is expected to continue keeping a close watch so that entrepreneurs may not prevent a new entrant from using the existing distribution channels or creating alternative channels. When a violation is detected, the Commission will eliminate it by strict and proper enforcement of the Anti-Monopoly Law.

Specifically, the Fair Trade Commission, after considering the policy recommendations of the International Comparative Study Group, and the problems revealed by the surveys on distribution of consumer goods, has decided to adopt the following competition policy approach:

(a) MANUFACTURER-AFFILIATED DISTRIBUTION CHANNELIZATION

Manufacturer-affiliated distribution channelization, ie manufacturers' development of organizational links or their strengthening of ties with their continuously trading wholesalers or retailers, may contribute to the rationalization of distribution process, and therefore, should not be regarded as inherently unfair. On the other hand, the Fair Trade Commission has regarded as unfair trade practices those cases where a powerful manufacturer requires that retail outlets shall not handle competitors' products as a condition of beginning transactions. This is likely to reduce transaction-opportunities for competitors. The Commission intends to continue to regulate such cases strictly and properly.

(b) REBATES

The term 'rebates' means the payment of money to customers outside the price structure of a particular item; these include what are referred to in Europe and the United States as 'volume incentives', 'cash discounts', 'advertising allowance', etc.

The rebate system fulfills various functions, including the promotion of flexible price formation in response to actual market conditions. Therefore, it cannot be regarded as a practice which inherently restricts market entrance. The

Fair Trade Commission will continue to implement careful surveillance and to control such cases where rebates have restrictive effects against new entries. For example, rebates paid by a powerful manufacturer may promote a tendency toward exclusive selling of that manufacturers' product by wholesalers and/or retailers.

(c) TRADE PRACTICES IN TRANSACTIONS WITH LARGE SCALE RETAILERS

1. Practice of returning unsold goods

In Japan, department stores and franchized stores employ a wide variety of a merchandise-purchasing systems. Sometimes, there is a practice to return unsold goods. Such a purchasing system decreases the purchaser's burden of risk associated with unsold goods and thereby makes it easier for them to try new sales items. Thus, in this respect, it increases competition by providing new items with easier access to retailers. Therefore, the practice of returning unsold goods may not be regarded as inherently unfair. However, such return of unsold goods may constitute an unfair trade practice in cases where a large scale retailer exploits its dominant bargaining position to return unsold goods in violation of terms of transactions previously agreed upon. This is especially true when the suppliers are forced to bear the entire burden of the unsold goods returned.

Thus, the Fair Trade Commission, aiming to prevent a powerful entrepreneur from making such unjust return of unsold goods in advance published guidelines entitled 'Viewpoints on the Unjust Return of Unsold Goods under the Anti-Monopoly Law' in April 1987. The guidelines showed that a justifiable return of unsold goods shall meet the following two requirements:

(a) a clear prior understanding should be reached between both parties at the time of purchase to the effect that return of the goods unsold is permitted under the terms of the transaction, and

(b) burden of risk from the return of the unsold goods is not to be disadvantageous to the other party in the light of other terms of the transaction.

2. Practice of seconding sales personnel

The practice of suppliers seconding sales personnel to the outlets of a large scale retailer such as a big department store to sell and promote the suppliers' products is fairly common. It is not something that is always done reluctantly by the suppliers under pressure from a large-scale retailer enjoying a dominant bargaining position. In fact, it is often the supplier that takes the initiative in order to get a significant promotional effect. Therefore, this practice also may not necessarily be condemned as restricting market entry in an unjust fashion. Nevertheless, there are cases where the practice results from a large scale retailer's abuse of his dominant bargaining position and thereby comes under one of unfair trade practices. In this regard, the Fair Trade Commission intends to continue regulating the practice and render guidance properly.

(d) PREMIUM OFFERS, REPRESENTATIONS AND ADVERTISING

1. *Premium offers made by new entrants (or on new products)*

Premium offers made by entrepreneurs are basically unregulated in the United States, while they are in principle prohibited in some of the European countries. Japan's regulations on premium offers lies between the two extremes and prohibits only excessive premiums.

Excessive premium offers are regulated by the Anti-Monopoly Law and the Premiums and Representations Law. They are based on the notion that excessive premium offers tend to work as unjust inducements to customers, hindering fair competition in terms of reducing prices and the improvement of the quality of goods or services, and impeding the interests of consumers in general.

On the other hand, premium offers may, depending on the manner and conditions of such offers, in some cases, provide the consumers with the opportunities to learn about new market entrants or new products, and increase the consumers' choice. Therefore, the Fair Trade Commission has given guidance as to the interpretations of relevant Laws, including the Premium and Representations Law. Entrepreneurs may use such premium offers to the extent that such offers do not bring about a risk of unjustly inducing customers.[8]

In this regard, the Commission clarified in May 1986 that offering of prizes (premiums) not exceeding one million yen at import fairs and similar events staged by official agencies such as embassies imposes no problem under the Anti-Monopoly Law or the Premiums and Representations Law when done with the aim of promoting consumers' interest in imported goods.[9]

Furthermore, the Fair Trade Commission has rendered guidance to some Fair Trade Associations to review the provisions of premium offer regulations in their Fair Competition Codes. So far, three Fair Trade Associations reviewed and relaxed their regulations on premium offers. They are the household synthetic detergent and household soap association, the cosmetic soap association and the magazine association.

2. *Comparative advertising*

Some foreign entrepreneurs claim that Japan's regulations on comparative advertising reduce the opportunity to convey information about imported products and hinder the effective advertising of imports.

The purpose of the Premiums and Representations Law, which is relevant in this respect, is to control the use of misleading representations that may affect the consumers' ability to select products. It does not prohibit comparisons with the competitor's commodities, in so far as it does not constitute misleading representations.

Proper comparative advertising promotes consumers' knowledge of qualities and features of the goods concerned, facilitates consumers' selection of

---

[8] 'Restrictions on Premium Offers to Consumers', FTC Notification 1 March 1977. Nakagawa, supra, p 196.
[9] See appendix 3.

commodities and may increase sales. This may be particularly true in the case of foreign products.

The Fair Trade Commission, in April 1987, published guidelines entitled 'Viewpoints on Comparative Advertising under the Premiums and Representations Act'.[10] The guidelines set forth the following three requirements for proper comparative advertising:

(a) the claims presented should be verified objectively;

(b) the facts and figures of the verification should be quoted accurately and properly; and

(c) the method of comparison should be fair.

The guidelines also refer to the approach to defamation, slander, and self-regulation by Fair Trade Associations and the media.

Furthermore, the Fair Trade Commission has rendered guidance to relevant Fair Trade Associations to review the provisions of comparative advertising regulation in their Fair Competition Codes. So far, the provisions of two codes, on fishing rods and agricultural machinery, were amended to allow comparative advertising.

3. *Representations of the country of origin*

In view of the growing competition between imported and domestic products, and also with the aim of ensuring consumers' selection of commodities, the Commission carried out a survey of the representations of country of origin on domestic wines from September to December 1986, and rendered guidance to the industry concerned.

(e) SOLE-IMPORT DISTRIBUTORSHIPS, MANUFACTURER-IMPORTS AND PARALLEL IMPORTS

In 1972, the Fair Trade Commission issued guidelines on sole-import distributorships—'Examination Guidelines on Unfair Trade Practices in Sole Import Distributorship Contracts.' Since then, the Commission has examined such contracts filed with it in the light of the guidelines and rendered corrective guidance to problematic contracts. Regarding manufacturer-import where the parties to a sole-import distributorship contract are competing goods manufacturers, the Commission has conducted specific examinations where a domestic party occupies either 25% or larger share or the largest share in the domestic market for the goods covered by the contract. The Commission has issued corrective guidance where necessary. Furthermore, the Commission has conducted a series of fact-finding surveys on sole-import distributorships and has taken necessary corrective guidance.

The Commission is to continue this approach. Concerning these problems, the Commission carried out a survey from a viewpoint of promoting imports of manufactured goods and to give consumers the gains resulting from the

---

[10] See appendix 3.

appreciation of the yen. This survey focussed on the roles and functions of sole-import distributors and parallel importers as well as their competition and distribution system in the import of 25 items of consumer goods such as Scotch whisky, chocolates, handbags, fountain pens, golf clubs and cars. The survey revealed the following facts:

Parallel imports occur where the domestic price level set by the sole-import distributor has been considerably higher than those in foreign markets, or where the sole-import distributor has limited the number of retail outlets. In some instances, the lower prices of parallel importers' goods lead to a reduction in the price level of the sole-import distributor's goods.

The findings show that parallel imports can promote competition by providing plural distribution channels and can function as a check on the prices of imports through sole-import distributors.

Based on the findings and a report on sole-import distributors and parallel imports prepared by a special study group the Fair Trade Commission, with the aim of preventing in advance sole-import distributors from employing conduct that may unreasonably impede parallel imports, published guidelines entitled 'Viewpoint on Unreasonable Obstruction of Parallel Imports under the Anti-Monopoly Law' in April 1987.

The guidelines specified six types of conduct that may unreasonably inhibit parallel imports. These included cases where a sole-import distributor conducts business with wholesalers on condition that they shall not sell the goods to retailers who handle goods imported by parallel importers.

The Commission is expected to keep a close watch over the conduct of sole-import distributors based on the guidelines in order to promote free and fair competition.

(f) INFORMATION NETWORK

Information networking has been increasingly employed in the Japanese distribution sector recently. This is generally designed to facilitate fast and accurate access to data regarding orders and sales of merchandise. This is done by linking manufacturers, wholesalers, and retailers through computer tele-communication networks. In this way, various manufacturers, wholesalers, and retailers involved are trying to rationalize their management and improve their sales efficiency. Therefore, such information networking should in principle result in such effects as enhancing efficiency and stimulating competition in the distribution sector.

Information networking can, however, have the effect of fixing and strengthening the already existing trade relations among manufacturers, wholesalers and retailers and its development may exert great influences on the relationships between manufacturers and distributors. Some kinds of data collected and communicated by information networking and their use may bring about competition policy problems such as resale price maintenance or abuse of dominant bargaining position.

Therefore, the Fair Trade Commission conducted fact-finding survey on the POS (point of sales information control) system and published the result in July

1984. The Commission will continue to monitor the installation and operation of inter- company information networks and will pay special care to ensure that such installation and/or operation does not impede market access.

Appendix 1

The Fair Trade Commission has powers including:

- (i) Receiving notice of mergers, international agreements or contracts, etc,
- (ii) Authorization of depression cartels, rationalization cartels, fair competition codes, etc,
- (iii) Compulsory inquiry,
- (iv) Publication of appropriate matters,
- (v) Submission of opinions to the Diet,
- (vi) Compulsory investigation of an alleged violation,
- (vii) Issuance of a recommendation for the elimination of an alleged violation,
- (viii) Holding hearings for an alleged violation,
- (ix) Rendering a recommendation decision, consent decision or hearing decision on an alleged violation,
- (x) Instigating criminal proceedings against Anti-Monopoly Law offences,
- (xi) Designation of unfair trade practices, and
- (xii) Rule-making on internal discipline, investigation and hearing procedures, etc.

Appendix 2

Viewpoints on unreasonable obstruction of parallel importing under the Anti-Monopoly Act

17 April 1987
Tentative translation
External Affairs Office
FTC

INTRODUCTION

In 1972 the Commission published *Examination Guidelines on Trade Practices in Sole-Import Distributorship Contracts, Etc.* The Commission has since advised against the inclusion in sole-import distributorship contracts of conditions that might be deemed unfair trade practices, and it has monitored the activities of sole-import distributors to ensure that these do not have restrictive effects on competition. It has also devised remedial measures to deal with violations of the Anti-Monopoly Act.

As stated in the *Examination Guidelines*, unwarranted actions to curtail parallel importing may constitute an unfair trade practice. When a sole-import distributorship contract includes elements that unfairly restrict parallel importing, the Commission advises the parties concerned to revise the contract. The sole-import distributor system and parallel importing have attracted widespread attention recently in the context of efforts to promote imports of manufactured goods and pass on to consumers the exchange gains resulting from the appreciation of the yen. The Commission has now conducted a survey of parallel importing. The results have prompted the Commission to publish its views on types of circumstances under which the activities of sole-import distributors that restrain parallel importing could be deemed violations of the Anti-Monopoly Act.

Under the sole-import distributor system, a foreign company gives a specific domestic distributor the exclusive right to import and sell a particular product. This system facilitates the entry of imported goods into the domestic market and thus can contribute to the promotion of competition. Depending on the market status of the import and the distributor and the behavior of the distributor, however, the system can also have restrictive effects on competition in the domestic distribution sector.

Parallel importing is a system whereby a third party imports the product covered by the sole-import distributorship contract via a channel other than that used by the parties to the contract. This leads to the development of multiple distribution channels and confronts the sole import distributor with competitive pressure in setting prices, thereby stimulating competition in the domestic market. Note that the following comments are based on the assumption that the goods imported via parallel importing channels are genuine products that do not violate trademark rights.

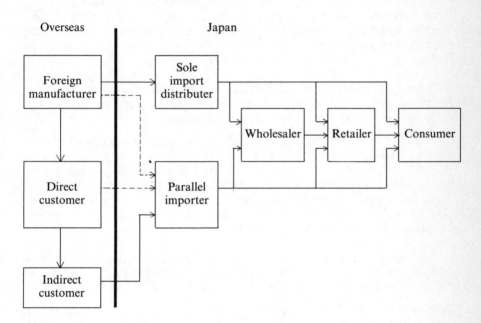

1. Activities that may unjustly restrain parallel importing

(1) When a Japanese parallel importer has approached a customer of a foreign manufacturer to purchase a product, and when the Japanese sole-import distributor attempts to prevent the foreign manufacturer or its customer from selling the product to the parallel importer (General Designations, Paragraphs 13 and 15).

In order for the sole distributor system to operate, it is necessary (1) for the foreign manufacturer to refrain from selling the product to a Japanese company other than the sole-import distributor and (2) for other direct customers of the foreign manufacturer to refrain from actively selling the product in the territory granted to the Japanese sole-import distributor. In general these requirements do not contravene the Anti-monopoly Act. Normally there is no violation of the Act if, for example, the foreign manufacturer sells the product directly to another Japanese company but is then forced to discontinue the sale in response to a request from the Japanese sole-import distributor.

However, the prevention of a parallel importer or individual from obtaining the product via an overseas distribution channel exceeds the scope of activities essential to the functioning of the sole distributor system. This may unjustly restrain the business activities of the foreign manufacturer or its customers and prevent transactions between foreign distributors and parallel importers in Japan. Thus, if a parallel importer in Japan approaches a foreign distributor that is a customer of the foreign manufacturer with a view to purchasing the product, and the Japanese sole-import distributor then calls on the foreign manufacturer or the foreign distributor to stop the transaction, this would unjustly hinder the business of the parallel importer and could be deemed unjust restraint on parallel importing.

(2) When a sole import distributor engages in transactions with a wholesaler or retailer on condition that it does not handle goods imported by parallel importers (General Designations, Paragraphs 11 and 15).

Wholesalers and retailers should be able to decide independently whether or not to handle goods imported by parallel importers. By engaging in a transaction on condition that the other party does not handle goods imported by a parallel importer, the sole-import distributor is reducing the trading opportunities of the parallel importer and may hinder transactions between the parallel importer and wholesalers and retailers. This could be deemed unjust restraint on parallel importing.

(3) When a sole-import distributor engages in transactions with a wholesaler on condition that it does not sell the goods to retailers who handle goods imported by parallel importers (General Designations, Paragraphs 13 and 15).

Wholesalers should be able to decide independently whether or not to sell goods purchased from the sole-import distributor to a retailer who handles goods imported by a parallel importer. By engaging in a transaction with the wholesaler on condition that the other party does not sell the goods to a retailer that handles goods imported by a parallel importer, the sole-import distributor is unjustly restricting the trading activities of the wholesaler and hindering transactions between the wholesaler's customer and the parallel importer. This may be deemed unjust restraint on parallel importing.

(4) When a sole-import distributor seeks the cessation of sales of parallel imports by distributors on the grounds that the parallel imports are imitation products in violation of trademark rights (General Designations, Paragraph 15).

The owner of a trademark can seek the cessation of sales of imitation products on the grounds that they violate trademark rights. When parallel imports of the same brand are being sold more cheaply than the products of the sole-import distributor, however, any accusation that the parallel imports are fakes, accompanied by demands that sales be called off, may harm the reputation of the parallel importer, even where the goods are genuine and can be verified as such, making retailers reluctant to handle the goods. Accordingly, when a sole-import distributor treats parallel imports as fakes without adequate reasons, basing the charge solely on an inexpensive price, and seeks the cessation of sales on the grounds that the products are in violation of trademark rights, this may be deemed unjust restraint on parallel importing.

(5) When a sole-import distributor attempts to buy up all parallel imports (General Designations, Paragraph 15).

When retailers attempt to sell goods imported by a parallel importer, sole-import distributors sometimes send representatives to the shop to buy up all supplies of the product in question. If products advertised as available to general consumers are bought up by the sole-import distributor, consumers who come to buy the product may complain that the retailer was engaging in false advertising, and the reputation of the shop may suffer. The buying up of parallel imports by the sole-import distributor also exerts psychological pressure on the retailer, who may decide not to handle parallel imports. For such reasons the buying up of goods by a sole-import distributor may be deemed unjust restraint on parallel importing.

(6) When the sole-import distributor refuses to provide repairs or other services for goods imported by a parallel importer (General Designations, Paragraph 15).

If goods imported by a parallel importer can be serviced only by the sole import distributor but the distributor refuses to provide service solely on the grounds that it did not itself handle the goods, the parallel importer may have difficulty selling the goods. A refusal to service parallel imports under these circumstances may be deemed unjust restraint on parallel importing.

2. Practices designed to maintain resale prices

In many cases retailers decide to handle goods imported by parallel importers because they find it difficult to discount goods supplied by sole-import distributors. Obviously the supply of goods to a wholesaler or retailer by a sole-import distributor on condition that the resale price be maintained could be deemed an unjust trade practice. If the sole-import distributor stipulates a resale price and, when this condition is not observed, resorts to such activities as the termination of deliveries, the reduction of rebates, the buying up of goods, the prohibition of trade sales, or the use of hidden marks to trace discounting channels, this may restrict free decisions on selling prices by wholesalers and retailers and could be deemed an unjust trade practice (General Designations, Paragraph 12).

Appendix 3

Viewpoints on comparative advertising under the Premiums and Representations Act

27 April 1987
Tentative translation
External Affairs Office
FTC

INTRODUCTION

In June 1986 the Commission clarified the basic implications of the Act Against Unjustifiable Premiums and Misleading Representations for comparative advertising. This interpretation is as follows:

a. Article 4 of the Premiums and Representations Act prohibits as misleading representation any description of the substance of a product or its terms of transaction that gives general consumers the erroneous impression that the product is overwhelmingly superior to or more advantageous than a competitor's product. The Act does not, however, prohibit or restrict all comparisons of products with those of competitors.

b. An appropriate comparative advertisement is one that provides general consumers with specific information enabling them to make accurate comparisons of the quality and sale terms of products of the same type, thereby assisting consumers' efforts to choose between products. Advertisements that exhibit the following characteristics may be deemed misleading representations on the grounds that they hinder accurate comparisons of product characteristics and prevent consumers from making appropriate choices:

(a) Where comparative claims are put forward that are either not proven or incapable of proof.

(b) Where comparisons emphasize aspects that are not essential to the selection of products by general consumers, or where comparisons are based on unfair criteria, including the arbitrary selection of the products to be compared.

(c) Where an advertisement does not provide consumers with specific information and merely defames or slanders a competitor or the competitor's product.

Comparative advertising has not been used extensively in Japan. In order that it may be used properly, the Commission deems it appropriate to outline its views on the types of situations in which such advertising would not contravene the Premiums and Representations Act. As an interim measure, therefore, it was decided to specify in greater detail the circumstances under which comparative advertising would be permitted under the Act, thus assisting in the prevention of infringements before they occur.

Advertisers intending to employ comparative advertising should do so in an appropriate manner with reference to the following guidelines.

1. Definition of comparative advertising

In the following, the term *comparative advertising* refers to advertisements in which comparisons (including implied comparisons) are drawn between goods or services (hereinafter referred to as 'products') and specific competing products, where the comparison is based on objective measurement or evaluation of the contents of the products or of the terms of transaction. When advertisements present comparisons in other forms, compliance or noncompliance with the Premiums and Representations Act will be determined according to the individual circumstances, with reference to the spirit of the following guidelines.

2. Basic interpretation

(1) RESTRICTIONS IMPOSED UNDER THE PREMIUMS AND REPRESENTATIONS ACT

Article 4 of the Premiums and Representations Act prohibits as misleading representation any description of the substance of a product or its terms of transaction that gives general consumers the erroneous impression that the product is overwhelmingly superior to or more advantageous than a competitor's product, or that the product is significantly better or more advantageous than it actually is.

(2) REQUIREMENTS FOR PROPER COMPARATIVE ADVERTISING

In order to avoid misleading representation as thus defined, comparative advertising must not contain material that is likely to create this type of erroneous impression among general consumers. Advertisements must satisfy the following three conditions:

(a) The claims presented must be proven objectively.

(b) The facts and figures of the proof must be quoted accurately and fairly.

(c) The method of comparison must be fair.

3. Condition 1: proof of claims

The general consumer will not normally be misled by comparisons based on objectively verified facts and figures. Accordingly, this type of advertisement does not constitute misleading representation. (Note: manifestly fanciful descriptions do not constitute misleading representation as long as their unreality is readily apparent to consumers, for there is little danger that ordinary consumers will be misled by material that is clearly fictitious.)

For objective proof of claims to be presented, the following comments should be taken into account.

(1) AREAS IN WHICH PROOF IS REQUIRED

The need for objective proof applies to all claims contained in comparative advertising. For example, in a comparative advertisement in which it is claimed that the results of a survey conducted in some city show that product A is superior to product B, the advertiser must (1) have conducted a survey in that city on the quality of products A and B and (2) have obtained survey results that support the claims in the advertisement.

(2) METHODS AND EXTENT OF PROOF

If there is an established method of comparison relating to the characteristics of the products (for example, the 10-mode test for automotive fuel economy), verification should be based on this method. If there is no relevant established method, the method used should be suitable according to generally accepted rules of common sense and empirical measurement (for example, random sampling survey procedures that evaluate large samples and are conducted in such a way as to exclude manipulation). The method must be used to an extent capable of verifying the existence of the facts claimed.

Judgments on the specific meaning of the phrases 'according to generally accepted rules of common sense and empirical measurement' and 'to an extent capable of verifying the existence of the facts claimed' should take into account the characteristics of the products compared and the scale and degree of influence of the advertisement. For example, if a claim about the strength of consumer preferences for the advertiser's product and another company's product is to be used for comparative advertising over a large geographical area, the claim will need to be substantiated by a survey that covers a large sample. By contrast, if a small company employs comparative advertising in a limited geographical area to sell a low-price product, such as soybean paste, a relatively small sample will be sufficient.

If objectively reliable facts and figures have been published by an official agency or made public in a pamphlet or some other form by the manufacturer whose product is to be compared, such data can be regarded as proven.

(3) SURVEY AGENCIES

It is preferable that surveys be conducted by third parties that are independent of the advertiser (for example, such official agencies as public testing and research institutions, or neutral private sector survey and research agencies), since such surveys can be regarded as objective. Results obtained by a third party connected with the advertiser may nonetheless be used as the basis for comparative advertising, provided that a suitable method is used to verify the claims.

4. Condition 2: accurate and fair quotation

Because consumers will not normally be misled by accurate and fair quotations of verified facts and figures, such quotations are not regarded as misleading representation.

For quotations to be made accurate and fair, the following comments should be taken into account.

(1) PROCEDURES FOR QUOTING SURVEY RESULTS

a. The quotation must remain within the scope of proven facts

For example, if a survey providing proof was carried out under limited conditions, the results must be represented as comparisons under limited conditions. A comparative advertisement could be deemed misleading representation if survey results were quoted in such a way as to imply applicability under all conditions when in fact they were obtained under limited conditions, since the evidence would not then be sufficient to support the claims made. An example would be a claim in a comparative advertisement for an engine oil intended for use in sub-tropical regions that the product is superior anywhere in Japan even though the comparative testing was only carried out under sub-tropical conditions.

b. Quotations of partial results must accord with the total survey results

For example, if a multiple item comparative test of many companies' products is quoted, the quotation might be deemed misleading if the advertiser has made an arbitrary choice of items to consider, assigned values to the items, and derived averages purporting to show the superiority of the advertiser's product.

(2) PRESENTATION OF DATA ON SURVEY METHODS

When comparisons are made by quoting survey findings, it is best when the advertisement contains information on the conduct of the survey, including the name of the survey agency and the date and location of the survey, for such information helps consumers to interpret the findings correctly. Provided that the survey method has been explained adequately, this information can be omitted for such reasons as insufficient advertising space. Even in this case, however, an advertisement could be deemed misleading if the omission of the name of the survey agency, the date of the survey, or other information tended to mislead consumers about the survey's objectivity or timing.

Consider an advertisement claiming that a survey has shown that 60 people out 100 consider product A to be better than product B. If the survey is fairly old and was carried out by the advertiser's company, any reference to the survey as 'a recent authoritative study' would create the impression that the survey was carried out recently by a third party. This could constitute misleading representation.

5. Condition 3: fair methods of comparison

Because consumers will not normally be misled if the method of comparison is fair, advertisements based on such comparisons are not regarded as misleading representation.

For methods of comparison to be fair, the following comments should be taken into account.

(1) SELECTION OF COMPARATIVE ITEMS FOR PRESENTATION

In general any aspect of a product can be used for comparison. Misleading representation may be deemed to have occurred, however, if comparisons based on specific items are presented in such a way as to imply that a product is superior in terms of overall functions or usefulness even though the items quoted are not very relevant to overall functions or usefulness. For example, an advertisement may be deemed misleading if it implies that the product advertised is revolutionary and new compared with the existing products of other companies, when in fact the improvement in the product is minor.

(2) SELECTION OF PRODUCTS TO BE COMPARED

In general any product that is in competition with the advertiser's product can be selected for comparison. Misleading representation may be deemed to have occurred, however, if the impression is created that the products compared are similar but in fact, according to generally accepted rules of common sense and business practice, they are not. For example, consider an advertisement comparing the luxurious interior fittings of a deluxe model of a car with the interior of another company's economy model. If no reference is made to the difference in class, implying that two cars of an equivalent class are being compared, the advertisement may be deemed misleading.

Misleading representation may also occur if the impression is created that the comparison relates to products that are still being produced and sold when in fact they are not. For example, an advertisement may be deemed misleading if the advertiser's latest product is compared with a competitor's product that is no longer in production without reference to that fact, thereby creating the impression that both products are new.

(3) PRESENTATION OF DRAWBACKS

In general it is not necessary to describe related shortcomings when presenting comparisons of product aspects. Misleading representation may be deemed to have occurred, however, if an advertiser intentionally fails to make explicit reference, or makes only an obscure reference, to an inferior feature that by law or custom should be disclosed and that is inseparable from the aspect of the product that is claimed as an advantage. This could mislead consumers about the general functions and usefulness of the product. For example, an advertisement for land may be deemed misleading if in a comparison of prices the advertiser fails to make reference to specific conditions, such as the presence of pylons for high-voltage power lines, that have lowered the value of the land advertised.

6. Defamation and slander

In comparative advertising, defamation and slander can be defined as statements intended to damage the reputation of a competitor or a competitor's products by deliberately emphasizing the weaknesses of the products without providing specific information on them. If a comparative advertisement contains defamatory or slanderous material that conflicts with the truth and may mislead general consumers, it may be deemed misleading representation.

Even when defamatory or slanderous statements are based on facts, an advertisement may be deemed misleading if it contains personal attacks or statements designed to harm the reputation of a competitor, or if the message of the advertisement creates a false impression among general consumers that the product referred to is of significantly less worth than is actually the case. Caution should be exercised with regard to such advertisements, since in some cases the penal Code or other legislation may be violated, and questions of ethics and propriety may be raised.

7. Self-regulation by Fair Trade Conferences and the media

The preceding comments are intended as general guidelines for interpreting comparative advertising under the Premiums and Representations Act.

The ideal way to establish normal business practices for comparative advertising and to ensure that such advertising is employed fairly, taking into account the characteristics of products and the scale and degree of influence of each advertisement, would be for Fair Trade Conferences and other bodies to draw up self-regulation criteria based on the preceding observations, and for these criteria to be applied where appropriate by such regulatory bodies as Fair Trade Conferences. The advertising media should also establish appropriate self-regulation standards for comparative advertising.

8. Other matters

Even though a comparative advertisement may be acceptable under the provisions of the Premiums and Representations Act, advertisers should be aware that other contents of an advertisement, such as the method used to quote survey findings and the classification of products in a comparison, may be prohibited under the Copyright Law or other legislation.

Index